KAAFJORD
Kola Inlet
PETSAMO
RVIK
MURMANSK

ARCHANGEL

MILES
0   800
0   1200
KILOMETRES

FINLAND

HELSINKI
LENINGRAD
OCKHOLM
TALLINN
ESTONIA
BALTIC
SEA
Volga
MOSCOW

RIGA
LATVIA
LITHUANIA
R U S S I A
KAUNAS
E.
PRUSSIA
G

WARSAW
Don
POLAND
Dniepr
CASPIAN SEA

LOVAKIA
BUDAPEST
NGARY
RUMANIA
BUCHAREST
LGRADE
BLACK SEA
GOSLAVIA
Danube
BULGARIA
SOFIA
TIRANĒ
ANKARA
I R A N
ALBANIA
RANTO
T U R K E Y
labria
GREECE

ATHENS
SYRIA
I R A Q
Rhodes
(ITAL.)
C.Matapan
CYPRUS
Maleme
Crete
A N E A N   S E A
PALESTINE
TRANS-
JORDAN

BENGHAZI
TOBRUK
ALEXANDRIA
of Sirte
Cyrenaica
EL ALAMEIN
CAIRO
SAUDI ARABIA
Y A
E G Y P T

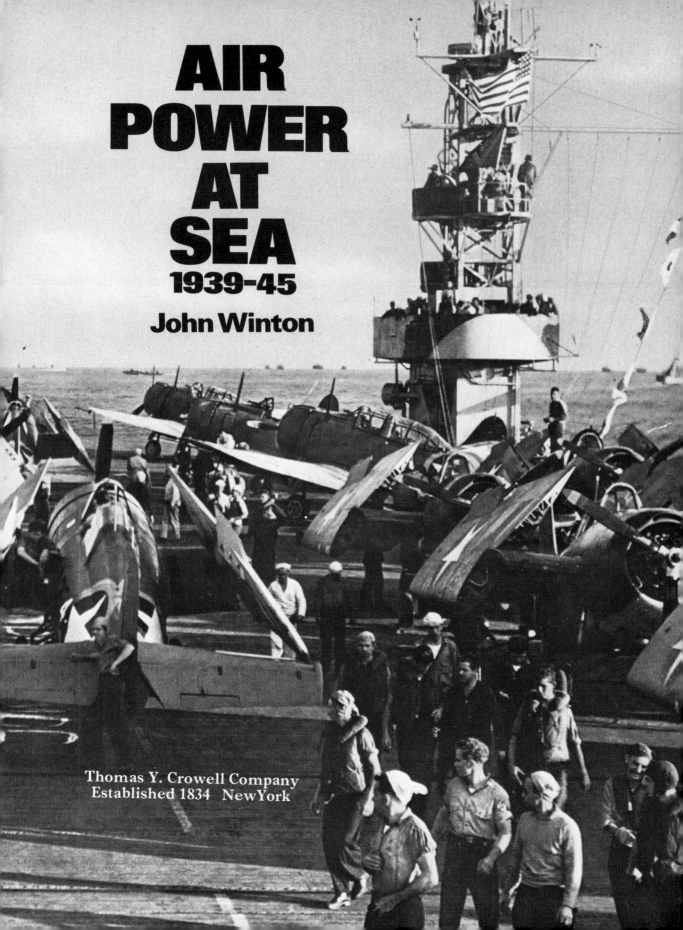

AIR POWER AT SEA
1939-45

John Winton

Thomas Y. Crowell Company
Established 1834   New York

Previous pages: **Douglas SBD Dauntlesses on an auxiliary aircraft carrier in the Atlantic**

First United States publication 1977
Copyright © 1976 by John Winton and Sidgwick and Jackson Limited
Maps copyright © 1976 by Richard Natkiel
Designed by Sarah Kingham
Cartography by Richard Natkiel

Acknowledgements
Aeroplane, The, *Wren cartoons:* 10; 24; 33; 39; 57; 66; 76; 82; 96; 111; 148; 180.
Associated Press: 12 bottom
Australian War Memorial: 51.
Bundesarchiv: 37 top left.
Fox Photos: 104–105.
Gaston Berelemont: 107 bottom.
Imperial War Museum: Front cover; 6; 8–9; 11; 12 top left; 12–13; 16–17; 18–19; 23 top and bottom; 25; 26; 28; 29; 30–31; 34; 40 top and bottom; 41 top and bottom; 42; 48 bottom; 50; 53; 56; 67; 72; 78; 79; 80; 83; 84 top and bottom; 86; 89 top and bottom; 90; 92 top and bottom; 95; 100–101; 102; 107 top; 108 top; 108–109; 110; 116; 118; 119; 121 bottom; 122–123; 126–127; 137; 152–153; 158–159; 164–165; 170–171; 171 top.
Paul Popper: 32.
Robert Hunt Library: 10; 14–15; 20; 22; 27; 37 bottom; 38–39; 43; 46; 47; 52; 64 bottom; 69; 74; 94; 97 bottom; 114–115; 124–125; 136; 154–155; 164 left; 168–169.
United States Air Force: 128; 133 top; 176–177.
United States National Archives: 2–3; 62–63 top; 97 top; 98–99 top and bottom; 112–113; 133 bottom; 146–147; 170 top.
United States Navy: Back cover; 37 top right; 44; 48 top; 49; 58; 60–61; 61 top; 62–63 bottom; 64 top; 65; 71; 87; 120–121; 131 top and bottom; 134–135; 139; 140–141; 145; 150–151; 156; 160–161; 162–163; 167 top and bottom; 172–173; 174–175; 178–179; 182–183.

'In peacetime, it may be frankly admitted, seaplanes available for picnics, shooting parties, or as substitutes for captain's galleys when lying at anchor far from shore, would be fun.'

Captain R.N., *c*.1930

Winton, John
Air power at sea, 1939-45.

Bibliography: p.
Includes index.
1. World War, 1939-1945 – Aerial operations.
I. Title.
D785.W53   940.54'4   76-41384

ISBN 0-690-01222-5

Printed in Great Britain.

Contents

1
Early Days: 1939-40

Norway, Spring 1940

Nobody really knew, in 1939, just how aircraft would perform in the coming war at sea. There were plenty of people in America and in Great Britain who thought – and said – they knew. The nautical counterparts of what was called the 'bomber lobby' said that the aircraft was invincible: 'the bomber would always get through'. But there were also a great many diehard conservative officers in every navy, Allied and Axis, who put their faith in the power of ships to defend themselves. For them, the aircraft was a passing irrelevance, somewhere between an adventure and a toy.

By 1945 there was no longer any doubt about what aircraft could do. Though certainly not invincible, the aircraft had proved itself by far the most powerful, most flexible, longest-ranging weapon ever used at sea. There was no end to the roles aircraft undertook. Carrier and shore-based aircraft made possible the defeat of the Atlantic U-boat. In the Pacific, carrier aircraft decided the fates of great battles in which no ship ever sighted an enemy. Deployed in huge numbers over vast stretches of ocean, aircraft were the spearhead of the triumphant Allied advance from Guadalcanal to Tokyo Bay. In a series of actions fought across the world, against *Bismarck* in the Atlantic, *Prince of Wales* and *Repulse* in the South China Sea, the Japanese carriers off Midway and the giant *Yamato* off Okinawa, aircraft showed that they could find and sink the largest ships at sea.

Ships were no safer in harbour. From Norway to Pearl

A Mosquito carrying out a rocket strike against shipping in a Norwegian fjord

H.M.S. *Furious* taking a huge wave
over her flight deck in heavy seas

A brilliant and now almost totally forgotten exploit by naval aircraft: the German cruiser *Königsberg* sinking alongside in Bergen Harbour after a dive-bomb attack by Skuas flying from the Orkneys, 10 April 1940

Harbor, from Taranto to Japan, aircraft with bombs and torpedoes damaged or destroyed ships lying in heavily defended positions. In amphibious landings from North Africa to Leyte, naval aircraft gave close support to the troops in the assault phase and afterwards held the ring until airfields could be secured ashore. Off the Philippines and Okinawa shore-based aircraft were finally used as suicide weapons, as desperate substitutes for a fleet at sea. Meanwhile, throughout the war and in every ocean, aircraft carried out the humdrum but vital duties of patrolling; looking for U-boats far out at sea, providing fighter cover over fleet, convoy or anchorage, taking reconnaissance photographs, reporting on the weather, or searching for survivors. As the war progressed, so too did the techniques and technologies of flying. As the number, variety and power of the weapons increased, so did the range, speed and load-carrying of the aircraft. In 1939 aircraft carriers mostly operated individually, and at best could only launch a handful of aircraft. By 1945, in the U.S. Navy's Fast Carrier Task Forces, fifteen carriers operated as one, and launched a thousand aircraft for a single strike. In every theatre of the war at sea the same lesson was there to be learned: air power properly used always brought immediate tactical and long-term strategic gains. The converse was also proved, again and again: lack of air power, or air power misused, always invited disaster.

In the Royal Navy these lessons had to be learned and painfully relearned. The Navy's problems stemmed from prewar days, when decisions about the policy, planning, equipment and training of a naval air arm were bedevilled by a very unlucky combination of circumstances. There was in the 1930s a general atmosphere of appeasement and a national reluctance to rearm. There had been a long and bitter inter-Service struggle, which only ended in 1938, to wrench back the control of the naval air arm from the Royal Air Force. There was, too, the Navy's own shortsighted failure to decide in good time what types of aircraft it needed most. And lastly, but having an important effect on naval thinking, there was a quite unjustified faith in the power of the new 'asdic' device to detect submerged submarines.

Those turned-up tips forbid mistake,
The howdah cab, the fillet's take,
Fin advanced and fish-like tail
Proclaim the Skua without fail.

The Blackburn Skua, the Fleet Air Arm's first operational monoplane, a two-seater dive-bomber/fighter which entered service in November 1938. Somewhat slow, and often outmanoeuvred by enemy types, the Skua was replaced by the Fulmar and the Sea Hurricane in 1941. Engine: one 905 h.p. Bristol Perseus XII radial. Span: 46 ft. Length: 35ft. 7in. Maximum speed: 200 m.p.h. at 6,500 ft. Operational ceiling: 15,200 ft. Normal range: 610 miles. Armament: four 0.303 in. Brownings, wing-mounted. The Skua could carry one 500 lb. SAP bomb

In 1939 the Royal Navy had six operational carriers of which only *Ark Royal*, completed in 1938, could be called modern. *Furious*, *Courageous* and *Glorious* had all been converted from cruisers at various times, during the First World War or just after it. *Eagle* had been converted from the Chilean battleship *Almirante Cochrane* in the 1920s. *Hermes* alone had been specifically designed as a carrier, but built as she was in 1919, by 1939 standards she was old, small, slow, and unarmoured. *Argus*, converted from the liner *Conte Rosso*, was used as a training aircraft tender ship.

The Royal Navy had no fast, manoeuvrable, single-seater monoplane fighter built for fleet service. Squadrons were equipped either with the Sea Gladiator biplane, a version of the R.A.F. Gloster Gladiator, or the Blackburn Skua/Roc, a single-engined monoplane dive-bomber/fighter with a crew of two. The standard torpedo-bomber reconnaissance aircraft was the Swordfish, the famous 'Stringbag', which had been designed and built as a private venture by the Fairey Aviation Company.

Nevertheless, the Navy went into the war with a rather better Fleet Air Arm than the country really deserved. The carriers had been in commission for some years and had experience in operating aircraft in various climates and weathers. There was a core of trained air and ground crews. Defensive and offensive tactics had been practised. There was an accumulated stock of shared knowledge and flying lore. In short, there was the nucleus of an effective, worldwide naval air arm of the future, if only its ships and men could somehow survive the inevitable shocks which come in the early days of any war.

This did not seem very likely, at first. Amongst the vestigial remains of First World War thinking which still prevailed in some quarters of the Admiralty was the notion that convoys were 'defensive' and therefore undesirable. Aircraft carriers should be employed 'offensively', as a kind of bold antisubmarine cavalry. In September 1939 the Home Fleet carriers *Ark Royal* and *Courageous* were dispatched on a series of punitive lunges around United Kingdom waters to any areas where U-boats had been reported. These tactics left the carriers dangerously vulnerable to counterattack. On 14 September, west of the Hebrides, *Ark Royal* was very narrowly missed by a bow salvo from U-39. The destroyers in the screen sank the U-boat, but it had been an anxious time, and worse was to follow. Three days later, south-west of Ireland, *Courageous* was hit by three torpedoes from U-29 and sank

Above: The German battlecruiser *Gneisenau* in action against the hapless aircraft carrier *Glorious* caught unaware and sunk off the Norwegian coast, June 1940

with the loss of her captain and 518 of her people. Although there was still a long way to go before a general acceptance of the principle that antisubmarine air power was far better concentrated around convoys, at least this first point was well taken and no more of these sorties were carried out.

Neither the German nor the Italian Navy ever had a carrier operational during the war. *Graf Zeppelin*, building at the outbreak of war, was still unfinished when she was eventually scuttled at Stettin in April 1945. But the Germans and the Italians were both able to use shore-based aircraft to great effect against Allied shipping in the European and Mediterranean theatres. However, at several crucial times senior officers in both Axis navies felt themselves to be at a great disadvantage in not having aircraft carriers. Likewise, their own thinking and their choice of operations were heavily circumscribed by their fear of Allied aircraft carriers. In the autumn and winter of 1939 the Royal Navy's carrier aircraft covered millions of square miles of ocean, searching for the enemy. This massive reconnaissance effort found very few actual targets, but it had a potent psychological effect on the enemy, who became convinced that the Navy's carriers were a brooding omnipresent force whose searching eye was quite likely to come up over the horizon at any time and anywhere. In that great 'fleet' so brilliantly conjured up by Churchill and the B.B.C. off the mouth of the River Plate in December 1939, it was the imaginary presence of *Ark Royal* that weighed most heavily on the mind of *Graf Spee*'s captain. It was no matter that *Ark* was actually hundreds of miles away. Langsdorff believed she could be there.

Above: H.M.S. *Furious*

Left: The first ship of the Royal Navy to be sunk by enemy action in the Second World War: the aircraft carrier H.M.S. *Courageous*, torpedoed and sinking, 17 September 1939

Norway, Spring 1940

For the Fleet Air Arm the Norwegian campaign opened with one splendid, although now almost forgotten, feat of arms. The German cruiser *Königsberg*, 6,000 tons, had been damaged in the attack on Bergen on 9 April and was reported to be lying immobilized in the harbour. In the early hours of 10 April seven Skuas of 800 Squadron led by Captain R. T. Partridge, Royal Marines, and another nine Skuas of 803 Squadron led by Lieutenant W. P. Lucy R.N., took off from the naval air station H.M.S. *Sparrowhawk*, at Hatston in the Orkneys. Each was loaded with a 500 lb armour-piercing bomb and the maximum load of fuel; for Bergen, at 300 miles, was only just within the Skuas' maximum return range.

They arrived above their target shortly after dawn, undetected. It was a beautiful morning, with a bright blue clear sky, the sun coming up like a blood-red orange, and the fjord a smooth steel mirror below. *Königsberg* was lying along-

The German cruiser *Königsberg* in a Norwegian fjord

The Gloster Sea Gladiator, converted for fleet service by fitting catapult points and an arrester hook to the R.A.F. fighter. The Sea Gladiator was the only single-seat fleet fighter at the outbreak of war, but it had virtually disappeared from operational service by mid-1941. Engine: one 725 h.p. Bristol Mercury VIIIA radial. Span: 32 ft. 3 in. Length: 27 ft. 5 in. Maximum speed: 257 m.p.h. at 14,600 ft. Operational ceiling: 33,500 ft. Normal range: 444 miles. Armament: two 0.303 in. Brownings on sides of front fuselage, one beneath each wing

side, looking like a slim leaf of silver. The Skuas, in line astern, were well into their dives before the flak opened up. None of the fifteen bombs dropped was more than fifty yards from *Königsberg*. Three were direct hits. Inside three minutes *Königsberg* was well ablaze, and after a large internal explosion she broke in half and sank. One Skua was lost on the run home down the fjord.

This was the first time that a major warship had been sunk by air attack. There were flurries of excitement in the major navies of the world. The Luftwaffe began to pay attention to specially trained dive-bombers for use against shipping. The Japanese added dive-bombers to the plans being formulated for the attack on Pearl Harbor. The Admiralty, however, withdrew the Skua from service early in 1941 and the Fleet Air Arm then had no dive-bomber until the curious Barracuda was introduced in 1943.

Meanwhile the campaign in general was not progressing

nearly as well. On 9 April, when the Germans attacked Norway, the only carrier with the Home Fleet was *Furious*, refitting on the Clyde. Her refit was hurriedly completed and she was dispatched to sea in such haste that she sailed for Norway without embarking her fighter squadron. This was like sending a battleship to sea without her armour plate. For the first fortnight of the campaign neither the fleet nor the army ashore had any fighter cover and as a result both were subjected to frequent and intense enemy air attacks.

It is probable that nobody at home, in the War Office or the Admiralty, really appreciated the full ferocity of the German air assault. During the fighting and in the evacuations that followed, the troops ashore and the ships at sea were constantly harassed from the air. Although the ships expended prodigious amounts of ammunition, guns alone were not enough protection. German aircraft sank the light cruiser *Curlew*, the destroyers *Gurkha* and *Afridi*, the French destroyer *Bison*, the Polish destroyer *Grom* and the sloop *Bittern*. They also hit the battleship *Rodney*, damaged *Furious*, the anti-aircraft cruiser *Curaçoa*, the destroyer *Eclipse* and a dozen more warships, store-ships and transports. The cruiser *Suffolk* came home with her quarterdeck awash, after seven hours of bombing attacks. The danger his ships ran of attack from the air was a continual worry to the C.-in-C., Admiral Forbes, affecting the dispositions of his forces, limiting the options open to him.

As the campaign went on, *Furious, Glorious* and *Ark Royal* tried to make up for the lack of shore-based aircraft, flying defensive sorties over the army ashore and the ships at sea, covering the evacuations and, whenever possible, striking at enemy shipping. In May *Furious* and *Glorious* ferried R.A.F. fighter squadrons to Norway. The first Gladiators from *Glorious* landed on a frozen lake where, after a very short time, the Luftwaffe found them and destroyed every one. Later squadrons had more luck, in fact the gallantry and devotion to duty of the R.A.F. and naval pilots were in shining contrast to the generally sorry handling of the campaign. Captain Troubridge's tribute to his own pilots in *Furious* could apply to them all: 'Their honour and courage remained throughout as dazzling as the snow-covered mountains over which they so triumphantly flew.'[1]

With better luck and better weather they might have done even better. On 11 April Swordfish from *Furious* flew to Trondheim to attack the heavy cruiser *Hipper*, but she had already sailed. Next day her aircraft attacked Narvik only to be foiled by bad weather. *Ark Royal*'s aircraft covered the evacuation of Narvik in June and on the 13th slung a Parthian shot by attacking enemy warships in Trondheim. *Scharnhorst* was hit by one 500 lb bomb. (Several Skuas were lost and

The old aircraft carrier *Eagle* converted from the Chilean battleship *Almirante Cochrane* in the 1920s

amongst those shot down, to become a prisoner of war, was Partridge. Lucy was shot down and killed in May.)

In Norway the Navy encountered determined enemy air opposition for the first time. The experience showed that it was not possible to maintain the Army on an overseas expedition, or even to operate ships for any length of time off an enemy coast, without proper and sustained air cover.

There was one last, cruel lesson from the Norwegian affair: an aircraft carrier not operating her aircraft is one of the most helpless things afloat. On 8 June *Glorious*, with two destroyer escorts *Ardent* and *Acasta*, was detached from the fleet to make her way home independently, because she was short of fuel. Earlier that morning she had successfully flown on R.A.F. Hurricanes and Gladiators from shore. None of their pilots had ever made a deck landing but they had chosen to take the risk rather than abandon their aircraft in Norway.

At four o'clock in the afternoon, funnel smoke from *Glorious* was sighted by the German battlecruisers *Scharnhorst* and *Gneisenau*, who were then steaming north hoping to find

Allied shipping leaving Narvik. *Glorious* was not flying reconnaissance patrols, nor maintaining fighter cover overhead. Maybe the large number of extra R.A.F. aircraft on board made normal deck-handling routines very difficult, or perhaps her captain, Captain G. D. D'Oyly-Hughes R.N., believed that the best way home was the straightest, without turning into and out of the wind to operate aircraft. Whatever the reason, *Glorious* was caught utterly unaware.

Scharnhorst opened fire at 28,000 yards and, as usual, the initial German gunnery ranging was magnificent. *Glorious* was soon hit on the bridge and on the flight deck. Marine Healiss, one of the guns' crews, said: 'The whole side of the *Glorious* seemed to cave in, leaving a choking cloud of smoke and a thunderous roar that echoed away to the darkening sky.'[2] Soon there was a serious fire burning in the hangar. More hits brought the ship to a standstill. At about 5.20 p.m. the carrier turned over to starboard and sank.

Her two destroyers had tried with great gallantry to save *Glorious*, both advancing through smoke-screens to attack *Scharnhorst* with torpedoes. One torpedo from *Acasta* actually hit *Scharnhorst*. But it was of no avail. Both destroyers were overwhelmed by the enemy's gunfire and both were sunk. The enemy did not stop to pick up survivors, and *Glorious*'s wireless had been wrecked in the first salvoes. Forty-two men from *Glorious* were eventually picked up, two from *Ardent* and only one, a leading seaman, from *Acasta*. Over 2,000 men from the three ships were lost.

Meanwhile, in the waters of the Skagerrak and Kattegat and off southern Norway, Allied submarines were enduring a prolonged ordeal. The submarine, as an arm, suffered its first defeat of the war. The interminable daylight hours of a Scandinavian summer, the sudden freshwater layers and fierce tidal rips, the minefields and the constant air and surface surveillance, all made submarine patrolling extremely hazardous. The Germans began to make good use of aircraft to cooperate with alert surface escorts, directing them to the datum of a submarine sighting, or occasionally making attacks themselves, using an airborne depth-charge (a weapon which Coastal Command still did not have). These tactics, coupled with intelligent use of radio direction finders and well-placed minefields, took a steady toll of Allied submarines. *Thistle*, *Tarpon* and *Sterlet* were lost in April, *Seal* and the Polish *Orzel* in May, the Dutch 0.13 in June. But the worst months were July and August, when *Shark*, *Salmon*, *Thames*, *Narwhal* and *Spearfish* were all lost. The Allies were forced to withdraw submarines from those coastal waters. Both sides seemed to wake up at the same time and realize the tremendous offensive potential of aircraft against submarines.

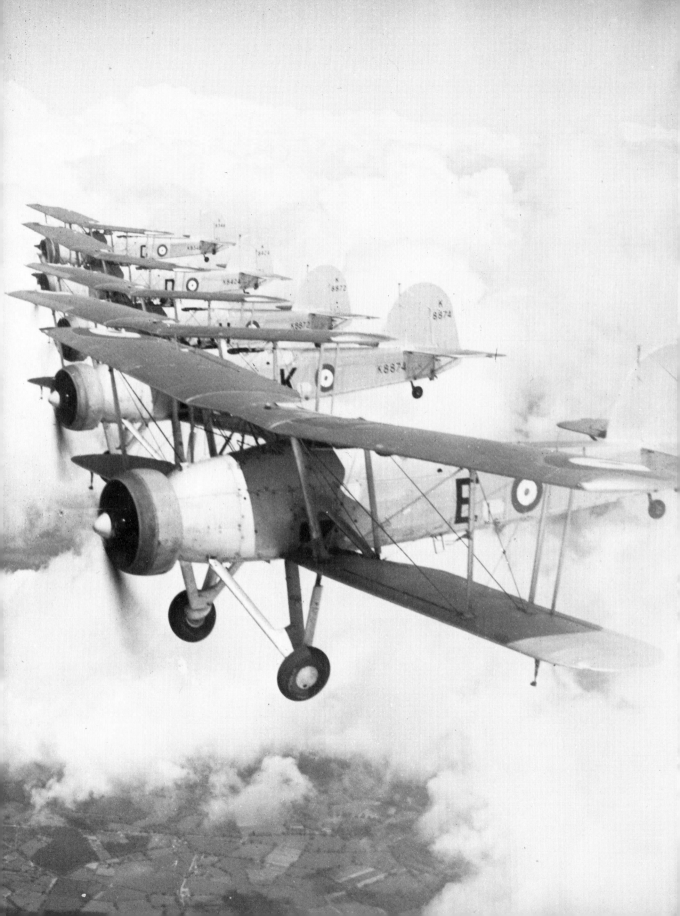

2 The Mediterranean: Taranto to Crete

The Fairey Swordfish, the famous 'Stringbag', which was the Fleet Air Arm's standard torpedo-bomber/reconnaissance aircraft in most theatres for most of the war, was still used operationally at the end of the war. Engine: one 690 h.p. Bristol Pegasus III M.3 radial. Span: 45 ft. 6 in. Length: 35 ft. 8 in. Maximum speed: 138 m.p.h. at 5,000 ft. Operational ceiling: 19,250 ft. Typical range: 546 miles. Armament: one 0.303 in. Vickers in upper engine cowling, one 0.303 in. Lewis or Vickers K in rear cockpit. The Swordfish could carry one 1,610 lb. torpedo, or eight 60 lb. rockets, or depth-charges

In the landlocked Mediterranean, control of the sea depended to a great degree on control of the airfields in Sicily, Sardinia, Libya, Cyrenaica, Crete, Greece and, most important of all, Malta. The fortunes of Admiral Sir Andrew Cunningham's Mediterranean Fleet tended to flow to and fro with the tide of the Army's success or failure on land.

Eagle joined the Mediterranean Fleet in May 1940 and she was followed late in August by *Illustrious*, the first of a new and larger class, fitted with an armoured flight deck and able to operate some thirty aircraft, including the new Fairey Fulmar two-seater fighter. Now, for the first few months after Italy entered the war, Cunningham enjoyed the rare luxury of a balanced fleet, in which capital ships and aircraft carriers complemented each other.

Cunningham took his chances. *Eagle*'s aircraft provided fighter cover, reconnaissance and gunnery spotting in the first engagement with the Italian battle fleet off the Calabrian coast on 9 July 1940. Swordfish also made an unsuccessful torpedo attack. The action was inconclusive, except that it reinforced the Italian Supermarina's already defensive attitude towards the Royal Navy in general and its carriers in particular. In July and August Malta-based Swordfish attacked shipping at Augusta in Sicily, at Tobruk, and at Bomba, west of Tobruk. After *Illustrious* joined, the fleet ranged freely from Rhodes in the east to Sfax in the west, its aircraft bombing airfields and harbours, laying mines in

Left: 'A victory very essential to England at this moment': the Italian battleship *Littorio* after the brilliantly successful Swordfish strike at Taranto, November 1940

Right: 'The Luftwaffe's revenge': the aircraft carrier *Illustrious* under very heavy dive-bombing attack west of Malta, 10 January 1941

Below right: Illustrious still under Luftwaffe attack alongside in Malta, 16 January 1941

coastal waters, strafing roads, railways and shipping.

Looking back later, that seemed a halcyon period, a superbly confident and successful demonstration of naval air power. The crowning achievement was the strike at the Italian battle fleet at Taranto which for a time decisively altered the balance of naval power in the Mediterranean and gave naval and air staffs all over the world fresh food for thought.

Taranto

Plans for an air strike at Taranto had been bandied about in the Fleet Air Arm as early as 1938. Admiral Cunningham longed for the chance of a decisive blow against the Italian battleships. But they were reluctant to go to sea. If they did go to sea, they seemed reluctant to leave the Gulf of Taranto. So, if they would not leave Taranto, they must be hit there.

The date was fixed for Trafalgar Day, 21 October, but a hangar fire in *Illustrious* caused a postponement. *Eagle* was also to have taken part but early in November defects in her petrol system caused by near misses from Italian dive-bombers became worse, and *Eagle* had to drop out. Five of her Swordfish, with eight pilots and eight observers, transferred to *Illustrious* for the strike.

On 10 November Glenn Maryland reconnaissance aircraft from Malta reported that the main Italian fleet, including at least five battleships, was lying in Taranto. On the evening of the next day, Remembrance Day, *Illustrious* was detached from the fleet and escorted by four cruisers and four destroyers steamed to the flying-off point which was some 170 miles south-east of Taranto.

The first strike of twelve Swordfish, led by Lt.-Com. K. Williamson R.N. took departure from the carrier at 8.57 p.m. and set course for Taranto. It was a fine night, with a three-quarter moon and thin cloud at about 8,000 feet. Six Swordfish were armed with torpedoes, four had bombs, and two had flares and bombs. The crews had trained hard for this operation. They were as fit, physically and mentally, as they could be. But their aircraft were unescorted, with darkness as their only defence. Each man sitting in his open cockpit, under the stars, was alone with his thoughts of what lay ahead. Lieutenant Maund, one of *Eagle*'s pilots flying a torpedo-bomber in the first strike, remarked on the cold at 8,000 feet, 'the sort of cold that fills you until all else is drowned save perhaps fear and loneliness. Suspended between heaven and earth in a sort of no-man's-land – to be sure, no man was ever meant to be here – in the abyss which men of old feared to meet if they ventured to the ends of the earth.'[3]

The harbour was protected by balloons and nets, and by

If you had been at Matapan
You'd know this biplane in the van,
For half the sea fights in the War
Have seen the Fairey Albacore.

The Fairy Fulmar, still a two-seater, but the Fleet Air Arm's first eight-gun combat aircraft. It saw its first operational service in *Illustrious* in the Mediterranean in 1940. A poor performer compared with land-based types, the Fulmar was superseded by the Seafire in 1942. Engine: one 1,300 h.p. Rolls-Royce Merlin 30 Vee type. Span: 46 ft. 4½ in. Length: 40 ft. 2 in. Maximum speed: 272 m.p.h. at 7,250 ft. Operational ceiling: 27,200 ft. Normal range: 780 miles.
Armament: four 0.303 in. Brownings in each wing. The Fulmar could carry one 0.303 in. Vickers in the rear cockpit, and also one 100 or 250 lb. bomb under each wing

guard-ships and shore batteries heavily armed with A.A. guns. The torpedo-bombers were briefed to attack the battleships lying in the outer harbour, the Mar Grande, while the bombers simultaneously attacked the cruisers and destroyers in the inner harbour of the Mar Piccolo. Soon after 11 p.m. the first line of flares drifted down the eastern side of the harbour and the Swordfish glided in for their torpedo attacks by the cold pale light, diving from 8,000 to 4,000 and finally to 30 feet above the water as they approached their targets. The defences had been given some two hours warning and were fully alert. The flare light was soon swamped by a hail of anti-aircraft fire, with 'red, white and green onions streaming past the cockpits'. The bombers jinked and swerved at mast-head height into the inner harbour. The aircrews could smell the acrid stink of the incendiary bullets, and their ears were deafened by the combined roar of the flak batteries on ship and shore. Maund could see 'a huge weeping willow of coloured fire showers over the harbour area; above it still the bursting HE shells and sprays of tadpole-like fire, whilst every now and then a brilliant flame bursts in the sky and drifts lazily down'.[4]

A second strike of nine Swordfish, led by Lt.-Com. J. W. Hale R.N. began flying off at 9.23 p.m. Five had torpedoes, two had bombs and two flares and bombs. One Swordfish was left behind on deck after a mishap but took off later. Another had to return prematurely with defects. But the rest could see the flames and flak of Taranto from sixty miles away. An observer wrote: 'I gazed down upon a twinkling mass of orange-red lights which I knew was a solid curtain of bursting shells through which we had to fly. It looked absolutely terrifying.'[5] The second strike plunged in through a renewed storm of fire to drop torpedoes, and dive-bomb ships and oil tanks beside the inner harbour.

The results went far beyond anybody's wildest expectations. The battleship *Littorio* sustained three torpedo hits which put her out of action for nearly a year. The older battleship *Caio Diulio* suffered one hit, but the resulting flooding was so serious that she had to be beached to stop her foundering. A third battleship *Conte de Cavour* also had one torpedo hit which sank her in shallow water; she was eventually raised, but took no further part in the war. The heavy cruiser *Trento* had one bomb hit, and there was more damage to destroyers and oil storage tanks in the inner harbour. Two Swordfish were lost, the crew of one being taken prisoner.

When *Illustrious* rejoined the fleet, Admiral Cunningham made her one marvellously laconic signal, 'Manoeuvre well executed'. A second strike had been planned for 12 November but was cancelled because of bad weather. Probably, too, Captain Boyd in *Illustrious* thought another operation so soon would be too much for his aircrews.

Taranto was, as Lord St Vincent said of his own battle in an earlier century, 'a victory very essential to England at this moment'. It must have convinced the last doubters of the power of aircraft at sea. It also suggested that against heavy ships the deadlier weapon was not the bomb, but the torpedo. Certainly, it made the Italians even more cautious. On 27 November, off Cape Spartivento, Sardinia, a powerful Italian force including two battleships retreated from a favourable tactical position on the threat of torpedo attack by *Ark Royal*'s aircraft.

By the end of 1940 Cunningham had established a clear moral and tactical ascendancy over the Italian Navy. But within two months the balance of power in the Mediterranean had tilted towards the Axis. As impatient with the Italian Navy's lack of success at sea as with the Italian Army's failure in Cyrenaica, the Germans transferred General Giessler's Fliegerkorps X, the Luftwaffe's anti-shipping specialists, from Norway to airfields in Sicily.

Ordeal off Crete, May 1941 : the cruiser *Gloucester* under air attack from which she later sank

The Luftwaffe's revenge

They caught *Illustrious* in the early afternoon of 10 January 1941, when she was escorting a Malta convoy, about 100 miles west of the island. The attack was as good a piece of flying as anything in the war. A pair of three-engined Savoia-Marchetti SM.79 bombers made a torpedo attack on the battleship *Valiant*, and while airborne Fulmars from *Illustrious* were at low level chasing them, and before fresh Fulmars could be launched and gain the necessary height, a strong force of Ju.87s and Ju.88s had gathered overhead.

The bombing attacks were of a higher standard of accuracy than anything the fleet had encountered before, and showed that there was now a new opponent in the field. In several attacks *Illustrious* was hit by six 500 kg armour-piercing bombs and near-missed three times. Had it not been for her armoured flight deck she must have been lost. The flight deck was pierced, the afterlift was blown out, the steering gear crippled and the hangar devastated. Serious fires broke out and there was severe underwater damage from the near-misses. Protected by her own Fulmars, which landed on Malta to refuel and rearm, *Illustrious* crept back to Malta, under her own steam but steering by main engines, arriving after dark. Her absence at once left the convoy vulnerable. The next afternoon the cruisers *Gloucester* and *Southampton* were both damaged by air attack, *Southampton* so badly that she caught fire and had to be sunk.

Sheltering in Malta, *Illustrious* was bombed and hit twice on 16 January, and again on the 19th. On the evening of the 23rd she successfully broke out and escaped to Alexandria. Her damage was much too serious to be repaired there.

A Seafire landing on *Formidable* with her arrester hook just taking the first wire

Eventually she steamed through the Suez Canal and on to Norfolk, Virginia, for a complete refit.

Eagle was now the only carrier with the fleet. She was old, unmodernized and in need of refit. Her relief was *Formidable* who arrived in March 1941, having come round the Cape and having been delayed by German mines in the Suez Canal. She was the second of the new class, with two squadrons of Fulmars, and two of the new Fairey Albacore three-seater TBRs, which were designed to replace the Swordfish and looked rather like them (in fact, both types served together and the Albacore was actually retired from service earlier than the Swordfish).

The surviving Italian battleships were still faster than all the Mediterranean Fleet battleships, and had a greater range than all except *Warspite*. The consummation Admiral Cunningham devoutly wished was therefore for his Swordfish or Albacores to slow down or, better still, immobilize the Italian heavy ships with torpedo hits and so allow his own heavy ships to catch up with them. For various reasons these hopes had been frustrated ever since the first brush with the Italian battle fleet off Calabria in July 1940. At the end of March 1941, however, the Mediterranean Fleet were given another chance.

Matapan

The Supermarina had at last yielded to German pressure to use heavy ships to interrupt the flow of Allied convoys to the army in Greece. On 27 March aircraft reconnaissance reported units of the Italian fleet at sea, steaming towards Crete. The Mediterranean Fleet sailed from Alexandria that evening.

Formidable flew off a dawn search the next morning, when the fleet was about 150 miles south of the eastern end of

Albacores ranged aft on the flight deck of *Victorious*; next astern is the battleship *Duke of York*. The Fairey Albacore was designed as a replacement for the Swordfish, but was actually retired from operational service first, in 1943, having taken part in the battle at Matapan, in the landings at Sicily and at Salerno. Engine: one Bristol Taurus II radial. Span: 50 ft. Length: 39 ft. 10 in. Maximum speed: 161 m.p.h. at 4,000 ft. Operational ceiling: 20,700 ft. Typical range: with torpedo, 930 miles. Armament: one 0.303 in. machine-gun in starboard wing, two 0.303 in. Vickers Ks in rear cockpit; one 1,610 lb. torpedo, or 2,000 lbs. of bombs

Crete. The searchers soon reported two forces of cruisers and destroyers some 100 miles to the north-west. Hopes began to rise in the fleet. Perhaps the Italians were out after all.

One of the forces sighted was thought to have been mistaken for Vice-Admiral Pridham-Wippell's cruisers, but all doubts were resolved at 7.45 a.m. when the look-outs in the cruiser *Orion* sighted smoke. It was the enemy. In classical cruiser style, Pridham-Wippell's ships withdrew to entice the opposition on to the heavy guns of the fleet.

The bait was taken up rather too enthusiastically and very soon Pridham-Wippell was being pursued and under fire from the battleship *Vittorio Veneto* on his port quarter and a force of three 10,000 ton heavy cruisers on his starboard. Matters might have gone hard for his ships, when help arrived in the shape of Albacores from *Formidable*, led by Lt.-Com. G. Saunt R.N., who at 11.27 a.m. attacked *Vittorio Veneto* with torpedoes. No hits were scored, but the battleship turned away and while turning to follow her the three heavy cruisers were also attacked by Swordfish flying from Maleme airfield, in Crete. But again, no hits were obtained.

Shortly after noon, *Formidable* launched another strike of three Albacores and two Swordfish, but before they could arrive *Vittorio Veneto* was bombed by R.A.F. Blenheims from Greece. Some of their bombs landed within fifty yards of the target, and added to the Italian Admiral Iachino's sense of grievance. Later, he was to complain bitterly that, while his

ships were sighted and then attacked by various kinds of Allied aircraft, they themselves were denied proper reconnaissance reports of the enemy's position and strength and were left totally undefended by fighters, either German or Italian, when under attack. At the same time as a torpedo attack by Savoia-Marchetti SM.79s on *Formidable* was just failing, a second bombing run by Blenheims coincided with *Formidable*'s strike of Albacores. The escorting Fulmars strafed *Vittorio Veneto*'s upper deck and gun positions, so distracting her that the Albacores were able to get in and score a torpedo hit, right aft. At the same time an R.A.F. high-level bomb exploded alongside. An observer saw 'smoke rings' puffing out of *Vittorio Veneto*'s funnels and her speed fell away. It seemed that Admiral Cunningham's heart's desire was about to be granted, and his adversary delivered into his hand.

But once again, it was not to be. *Vittorio Veneto* managed to improve her speed and draw away, while the pursuers had been hampered ever since leaving Alexandria by the slow speed of *Warspite*; mud and sand had entered her main condensers while leaving harbour and she could do no more than 22 knots at first and later, after urging, 24. At teatime *Formidable* launched yet another strike which was joined en route by two more Swordfish from Maleme. They missed the battleship but hit the cruiser *Pola* and stopped her dead in the water.

Iachino had had no reports at any time during the day that heavy units of the Mediterranean Fleet were anywhere near him. The nearest reported enemy ships were seventy-five miles astern and these Iachino assumed were either the cruisers he had engaged that morning, or destroyers. Lack of proper air reconnaissance led him to make a fatal decision. He ordered the heavy cruisers *Zara* and *Fiume* to turn back and assist their stricken sister ship *Pola*.

Forewarned in plenty of time by radar, Cunningham's heavy ships caught their opponents completely by surprise. A destroyer's searchlight illuminated *Zara* and *Fiume* with their guns still trained fore and aft. Both were sunk by the combined gunfire of *Warspite*, *Valiant* and *Barham*. Destroyers later found and dispatched the still stationary *Pola* with torpedoes. So, in this night battle of Cape Matapan, the Italians lost three heavy cruisers and, for good measure, two destroyers – *Alfieri* and *Carducci*.

Matapan was a magnificent victory, but once again the Luftwaffe took their revenge on *Formidable* just as they had done on *Illustrious*. On 26 May, during the battle for Crete, *Formidable* launched a dawn strike of four Albacores and four Fulmars to bomb and strafe the airfield at Scarpanto, an island east of Crete, where many of the aircraft harassing

Admiral Sir Andrew Cunningham, C.-in-C. Mediterranean Fleet, the finest sea captain of the Royal Navy in the Second World War

Allied troops in Crete were based. At 1.25 that afternoon *Formidable* was found and attacked by about thirty Stukas flying from North Africa. By coincidence these dive-bombers were from II Group of the 'Immelmann' *Stukageschwader* (Dive-bomber Wing) which had also attacked *Illustrious*. Soon, *Formidable* was following the same melancholy track: two hits with 500 kg armour-piercing bombs, severe under-water damage from a near miss, retreat to Alexandria, and so through the Suez Canal to the United States.

Crete

Formidable's departure meant that there would be no carrier operating regularly in the eastern and central Mediterranean for over two years. Air cover for the fleet was provided by No. 201 Naval Co-operation Group of the Middle East Air Force, using disembarked naval squadrons as part of their force. With the best will in the world, aircraft controlled by the R.A.F. could never give Cunningham the intimate and responsive action that an aircraft carrier under his own command could provide.

The Navy had no carrier for the evacuation of Crete. Cunningham well knew the dangers of operating ships inshore with no close air cover, but without hesitation he decided that the Army must be taken off. The soldiers could not be abandoned to their fate, whatever the cost in ships and men might be. As he said himself: 'It takes the Navy three years to build a ship, it would take three hundred to rebuild a tradition.'[6]

Off Crete the Navy suffered its worst ordeal by air attack of the whole war. In one day, 22 May, the cruisers *Gloucester* and *Fiji*, and the destroyer *Greyhound* were lost to air attack. The next day, *Kelly*, *Kashmir* and *Kipling* of the 5th Destroyer Flotilla were returning from a bombardment of Maleme airfield, now in German hands, when shortly after breakfast they were caught by a pack of Stukas. *Kashmir* was soon sunk and *Kelly* followed. *Kipling* stayed to pick up survivors and eventually reached Alexandria with 279 survivors, having dodged over eighty near misses, thus vindicating the decision of Captain (D), Lord Louis Mountbatten, to stay to pick up all they could. 'I felt it would be better for us all to be sunk together than to leave any of our flotilla mates struggling helplessly in the water without any prospect of being saved.'[7]

Another black morning was 29 May, when the evacuation was in full swing. The destroyer *Imperial*, which had been near-missed the day before, broke down when her steering gear jammed. Another destroyer *Hotspur* was sent back to take off her soldiers and sink her. In a second attack the destroyer *Hereward* was badly damaged, left behind, and lost. The cruisers *Orion*, *Ajax* and *Dido*, with hundreds of exhausted troops on board, came under very heavy attack just after daybreak. *Dido* was hit and damaged but the worst incident happened in *Orion*. A bomb penetrated to a messdeck crowded with soldiers and wreaked fearful devastation. The Captain was killed, with many other officers and men of *Orion*'s ship's company. As Cunningham had feared, the Navy paid a very heavy price to uphold their tradition, but their reward was in the relieved faces of the soldiers and their sublime faith that the Navy would never let them down and would be there, as expected, on the day.

Force H

While Cunningham's fleet suffered in the east, Force H held the ring in the western Mediterranean. Force H had been constituted on 28 June 1940, under the command of Admiral Sir James Somerville, to fill the vacuum caused by the defection of the French Fleet after the fall of France, and to prevent major units of the Italian Fleet moving westwards.

Force H was a balanced fleet in miniature, what was later called a Task Force, centred on the carrier *Ark Royal*, with capital ships, cruisers and escorting destroyers. *Ark Royal*'s aircraft took part in the immobilization of the French Fleet at Oran in July, and in the abortive landing at Dakar in September. The Dakar expedition, though militarily and politically misconceived, was the first occasion when a carrier provided the sole air support for an amphibious landing. Some valuable lessons were learned. One carrier alone simply could not provide reconnaissance, fighter defence and torpedo strikes (in fact, *Hermes* should have taken part but was damaged in a collision a month earlier). Swordfish were very slow and vulnerable for daylight attacks against alerted targets. As for the ponderous Skuas, they were easily outperformed by the Vichy French Morane Saulnier 406 and Curtiss Hawk 75 fighters.

Force H demonstrated superbly well the great flexibility and striking power of any force which included carriers. After the action off Spartivento in November 1940, *Ark*'s aircraft played their parts in a variety of operations: striking at the Tirso Dam in northern Sicily in February 1941, spotting for the guns of the fleet off Genoa, laying mines at La Spezia, patrolling west of Gibraltar to prevent German heavy ships breaking out of Brest, and in April and May ferrying fighters to Malta. Less than six days after flying off some of these reinforcements, *Ark* was taking part in another drama, played out in the Atlantic 2,000 miles to the west.

A fighter of the Fleet –
One of the élite –
Of Stukas it's a harrier,
The Fulmar from the carrier.

3
Bismarck

The pursuit and destruction of the German battleship *Bismarck* in the Atlantic in May 1941 was the prime example of maritime air power complementing surface force, to find, fix, and strike at an enemy. Aircraft assisted in the task of sighting and shadowing *Bismarck*. Reconnaissance aircraft resighted her when she had been lost for hours and might have escaped. Torpedo-bombers hit and disabled her, bringing her to action with surface ships at a time when, again, she might have got away.

After months of intensive training in the Baltic, *Bismarck* and the heavy cruiser *Prinz Eugen* sailed from Gdynia on 18 May for an extended sortie against Allied shipping in the Atlantic. When intelligence sources reported their sailing on the 20th, Coastal Command mounted searches along the Norwegian coast which, on the 22nd, revealed that the two ships had reached Korfjord, a few miles south of Bergen. The next day a target-towing Maryland with a very experienced observer, Cdr. G. A. Rotherham R.N., on board flew from Hatston to search Korfjord and Bergen Fjord. In spite of bad weather, with thick cloud almost down to sea-level, and fierce flak, the Maryland made a thorough search. Both ships had sailed. The Maryland's radio had failed, so the telegraphist air gunner passed the message back to Hatston on the target-towing frequency, and so to Admiral Tovey, the C.-in-C. Home Fleet, and the Admiralty. One of the greatest hunts in the Navy's history was on.

Bismarck **photographed by R.A.F. reconnaissance in Bergen Fjord, 21 May 1941**

Opposite above:

Left: Admiral Lutyens

Right: Consolidated PBY Catalina flying boat, an invaluable aircraft for long-range ocean search and for attacks against surfaced U-boats. Nearly four thousand of them were built, and they served all over the world with Coastal Command, the U.S.A.A.F., the U.S. Navy Air Force, the Royal Canadian Air Force, and in the U.S.S.R. Engines: two 1,200 h.p. Pratt and Whitney R-1830-S1C3-G Twin Wasp radials. Span: 104 ft. Length: 63 ft. 10½ in. Maximum speed: 190 m.p.h. at 10,500 ft. Operational ceiling: 24,000 ft. Maximum range: 4,000 miles. Armament: six 0.303 in. Vickers, one in bow, two in each side blister, one in ventral tunnel aft of hull step. The Catalina could also carry up to 2,000 lbs. of bombs, or depth-charges

Aircraft took a part again late on 24 May. By that time much had happened. *Bismarck* and *Prinz Eugen* were sighted on the evening of the 23rd and shadowed by the cruisers *Norfolk* and *Suffolk* in the Denmark Straits. In the early hours of the next day the German ships shocked the world by sinking the battlecruiser *Hood*, perhaps the best-known warship of prewar days, who went down with only three survivors from a ship's company of 1,419 officers and men. *Bismarck* also hit the new battleship *Prince of Wales* and forced her to retire. *Prince of Wales* was hampered by machinery troubles (her forward turret could only join in the first salvo) but she still managed to score two hits herself on *Bismarck*. The damage done was physically only superficial, but it did mean that *Bismarck* could not use about 1,000 tons of her fuel. The German Admiral Lutyens decided to abandon the sortie into the Atlantic and make for France instead. *Bismarck*'s run southward, still shadowed by *Prince of Wales* and the cruisers and by Coastal Command, brought her within range of the 2nd Cruiser Squadron and the aircraft of the new carrier *Victorious*. There seemed no sign that the action with *Prince of Wales* had slowed *Bismarck* down. A torpedo strike by aircraft from *Victorious* seemed the only hope. So events and plans at sea and in the air ran together.

As evening drew on and *Victorious* prepared to launch aircraft, *Bismarck* suddenly altered course to the west and had a short sharp gun engagement with the cruisers. This was to cover the withdrawal of *Prinz Eugen*, who was to proceed independently to France. But it also opened the distance from *Victorious*, so that she could not intercept until much later in the day, and at further range than her commanding officer, Captain H. C. Bovell R.N., preferred for his inexperienced aircrews. However, Admiral Curteis, commanding the 2nd Cruiser Squadron, decided that he could wait no longer and at ten o'clock that evening *Victorious* flew off nine Swordfish of 825 Squadron, led by Lt.-Com. Eugene Esmonde, who had been a survivor of *Courageous*. Three Fulmars were also launched, for shadowing duties.

Esmonde's squadron had embarked in February but they were still raw and inexperienced in operational flying. Some of his crews had only been on board a week and some had only landed on a flight deck a few times. In that high latitude it was not dark until after midnight, but flying conditions were otherwise appalling. A very strong north-west wind had kicked up a thirty-foot swell. Lowering rain clouds lashed the flight deck with heavy squalls. Aircraft and men were soaked by rain and spray. However, all nine took off safely and flew away into a darkening sky. They had 120 miles to go. The thoughts of everybody in *Victorious*, in Tovey's flagship *King George V* far

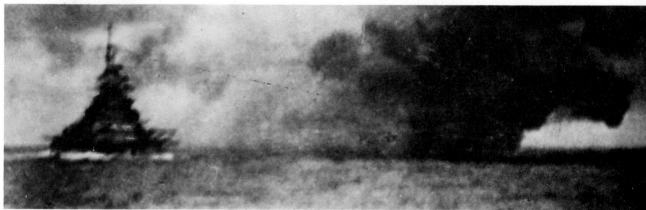

Above: Bismarck firing at *Hood,*
24 May 1941

away, and in the Admiralty at home, went with them. Some of those in *Victorious* wondered if they would ever see them again.

The visibility grew worse, but the Swordfish were fitted with the new ASV (air to surface vessel) radar and at 11.27 p.m. a contact was obtained. It was *Bismarck,* and the ship herself was soon sighted, at a range of about twenty miles. Esmonde retreated into cloud while he closed the target. When he emerged he could see only the shadowing cruisers *Norfolk* and *Suffolk* who gave him, and each flight of Swordfish as they passed, the correct bearing for *Bismarck.* Esmonde went back into cloud again and had another radar contact. This was the U.S. Coastguard cutter, *Modoc.* But *Bismarck* was in sight, only eight miles away to the south.

Bismarck's gunners were now thoroughly alerted and the Swordfish had to make their attacks through very accurate flak. Esmonde's aircraft was hit at four miles. One Swordfish was separated from the rest but the others pressed on. The

Lt.-Com. Eugene Esmond, second from left, who led the Swordfish attack on *Bismarck* from *Victorious* on 24 May 1941, and who later won a posthumous Victoria Cross for his gallant attack on the German heavy ships during the 'Channel Dash', February 1942, seen here with members of 825 Squadron

observers on *Bismarck*'s spotting positions were amazed to see such obsolete-looking biplanes having the nerve, as one of the gunnery officers said, to attack 'a fire-spitting mountain like *Bismarck*'.[8] Seven Swordfish, including Esmonde, attacked from the port side but one flew round to the starboard side and it was this aircraft which, shortly after midnight, scored a hit. One of the shadowing Fulmars reported a 'great column of dense smoke rising from the starboard side'.[9]

By the time the Swordfish had returned to *Victorious* it was dark and none of Esmonde's pilots had made a night landing before. The homing beacon faded out, making their approach all the more difficult. Captain Bovell had all the landing lights switched on and shone his largest searchlight until an alarmed Admiral Curteis ordered him to put them out. Whereupon

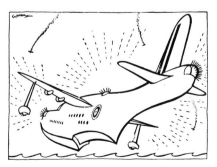

Reconnaissance sounds inoffensive,
Like a gull sailing high o'er the sea.
But the Sunderland's prickly defensive
Makes patrolling a porcupine's spree.

Captain Bovell began a very long signal with a very bright signalling lamp. Happily, the nine Swordfish landed on safely, although two of the Fulmars were lost.

Shortly after 3 a.m. the next morning luck turned *Bismarck*'s way. Perhaps over-confident after so long shadowing, *Suffolk* returned from the outward leg of a zigzag and failed to relocate *Bismarck*. She was gone, having chosen her moment to alter sharply to the west and increase speed. *Bismarck* was lost, and she stayed lost for that day and into the next. Hopes sank lower every hour. There was nothing now to prevent *Bismarck* reaching Brest, her assumed destination.

At 10.30 a.m. on 26 May *Bismarck* was found again, by a Catalina flying boat of Coastal Command piloted by Flying Officer D.A. Briggs of 209 Squadron (his co-pilot was Ensign L. Smith, an American, although America was still neutral). *Bismarck* was some 690 miles west-north-west of Brest, her speed apparently undiminished and her gunners as aggressive as ever. When the Catalina inadvertently flew too close to her, Smith said he could see the flak bursts very close, and hear fragments of shrapnel hitting the Catalina's hull. Force H, including *Ark Royal*, had been steaming up from Gibraltar during the night. Two of *Ark*'s Swordfish found *Bismarck* shortly after the Catalina's report, and took over the watch. *Bismarck* was firmly held again.

The quarry might have been found again but she was now so far south and still going so well that the only hope of catching her, and that hope was very faint, lay in a disabling strike by *Ark Royal*'s aircraft.

At 1.15 p.m. the cruiser *Sheffield* was detached from Force H to close *Bismarck* and shadow her. Unfortunately the signal reporting this had not been deciphered in *Ark Royal* before the Swordfish were launched at 2.15. Fourteen Swordfish took off, flying out over a stormy sea in a rising gale. It was still raining hard and the flight deck was pitching violently, plunging and swooping up again as much as sixty feet at a time.

A radar contact was obtained at 3.50 and the Swordfish attacked. It was not *Bismarck* but *Sheffield*, who with great forebearance refrained from firing and took drastic avoiding action. All the torpedoes missed or, being fitted with magnetic pistols, exploded harmlessly.

Something was learned from this humiliating failure. When a second strike was launched at 7.10 p.m. the Swordfish carried torpedoes with contact firing pistols and shallower depth running settings. This time there was no mistake. Flying in poor light, rain squalls and intense flak the Swordfish began their runs at 8.47 and the attacks were spread over about forty minutes. One Swordfish of 810 Squadron dropped

Right: Force H off Gibraltar. The cruiser *Sheffield* (top), the aircraft carrier *Ark Royal* (centre) and the battlecruiser *Renown*

Below: Ark Royal torpedoed and listing with a destroyer going alongside to take off her ship's company, 14 November 1941

Above: H.M.S. *Victorious* with
Corsairs ranged on deck and the
ship's company aft for Sunday
morning church service

Right: An Albacore taking off from
Victorious. Ahead is the battleship
H.M.S. *King George V*

Above: Admiral Sir John Tovey, C.-in-C. Home Fleet

Opposite: Ark Royal torpedoed and listing, survivors being taken off. Mediterranean, November 1941

her torpedo on *Bismarck*'s port bow at a range of 800 yards. Her observer, Sub.-Lt. C. E. Friend R.N., said that '*Bismarck* impressed me at first by her great size. She looked bigger than any warship I had seen before, as indeed she was. She had a wicked look because unlike British battleships of the time, which had plenty of space amidships between funnels and bridge, all her upperworks were together, giving her a humped appearance.'[10]

Bismarck's fire was still heavy and very accurate. Friend saw her decks seem 'to explode into crackling flame as she opened fire on us. The sea around was lashed by various sizes of shot and fragments and explosions were filling the air around us.'[11] Their torpedo hit amidships when, Friend noticed, *Bismarck* seemed to be in a wide slow turn. This was due to a second hit, of vital importance. It crippled *Bismarck*'s steering gear, jamming her rudder hard over and damaging her propellers. By a miracle of luck the Swordfish had scored the only possible kind of hit which could have delayed *Bismarck*. Her technical staff and divers worked frantically to repair the damage, but did not succeed. *Bismarck* continued to steam in slow helpless circles. She was harried all night by the 4th Destroyer Flotilla and, on the morning of 27 May, delivered up to the heavy guns of *King George V* and *Rodney*. Smashed into a burning shambles, *Bismarck* was eventually sunk at 10.40 a.m. by torpedoes fired from the cruiser *Dorsetshire*.

Loss of *Ark Royal*

Since the beginning of the war, *Ark Royal* had borne a charmed life. She had often been attacked by the enemy. German broadcasts, especially by the egregious Lord Haw-Haw, had often claimed her sunk. Her luck held in the *Bismarck* episode. On the evening of 26 May she and *Renown* had actually crossed the periscope sights in a perfect firing position of U-556, who however had expended all her torpedoes. *Ark*'s good fortune lasted until 13 November 1941 when she was torpedoed by U-81 when returning from escorting yet another convoy to Malta. It was only one torpedo hit and she should have survived, though listing and temporarily losing power. She was taken under tow, but by mischance and faulty damage control she sank lower in the water and eventually turned over and sank at 6.13 a.m. on the 14th, when she was only twenty-five miles from Gibraltar. All her company except one survived, and among them was Lt.-Com. Esmonde. *Ark Royal*'s loss was a great blow to national self-esteem. She had seemed unsinkable. Her going was like the end of an era.

4
Japanese Victories

Pearl Harbor

It was left to the Imperial Japanese Navy to employ naval air power in the most spectacular manner, for strategic ends and on a global scale. By 1941 American economic sanctions against Japan, especially the embargo on oil, had brought Japan to the point where she must either go to war, or lose face by retreating from her prewar conquests on the Chinese mainland. Japan's war objectives were the rich resources of South-East Asia, including the oilfields of Indonesia. Her main opponent was the United States. Her best defence was offence and her best mode of attack was a sudden pre-emptive strike on the U.S. Fleet to prevent its ships interfering with the Japanese invasions of South-East Asia. Her aircraft carriers gave Japan the means of delivering such a blow at very long range. It would be a gamble. Many high-ranking Japanese officers were well aware of that, including Admiral Isoruku Yamamoto, C.-in-C. of the Combined Fleet, who prophesied that for the first six months of the war Japanese forces would run amok. After that, Yamamoto was not so sure.

Part of the success of the Japanese plan for an attack on Pearl Harbor lay in its sheer unexpectedness. Nobody believed that the Japanese could simultaneously strike at Honolulu in the east, and the Philippines and Malaya in the west. Though there was ample intelligence evidence of Japanese intentions, there was still a tendency in America (and in the United Kingdom) to regard the Japanese as a

Pearl Harbor: the battleship *Pennsylvania* and the destroyers *Cassin* and *Downs* damaged in dry dock

Above: Zekes warming up on the flight deck of *Akagi* before Pearl Harbor. The Mitsubishi A6M Zero-Sen, known to the Navy as the 'Zeke', was in 1941 the best fighter in the East. It was fast and highly manoeuvrable, but its lack of armour and its readiness to catch fire made it more vulnerable as the war progressed. Engine: one 940 h.p. Nakajima Sakae 12 radial. Span: 39 ft. 4½ in. Length: 29 ft. 8¾ in. Maximum speed: 332 m.p.h. at 14,930 ft. Operational ceiling: 32,810 ft. Normal range: 1,162 miles. Armament: two 7.7 mm. type 97 machine-guns in upper front fuselage, one 20 mm. type 99 cannon in each wing. The Zeke could carry one 132 lb. bomb under each wing

somewhat backward, imitative Asiatic race with short sight and shorter legs.

The Japanese Navy had two large new aircraft carriers, *Zuikaku* and *Shokaku*, both of 20,000 tons, carrying some eighty aircraft, and completed in 1941. Two more large 27,000 ton carriers, *Akagi* and *Kaga*, had been converted in the late 1920s from a battlecruiser and a battleship respectively. Two smaller carriers, *Hiryu* and *Soryu*, of 10,000 tons, had been built in the late 1930s. These six carriers had some 450 aircraft embarked. In the Mitsubishi A6M Zero-Sen (codenamed 'Zeke') the Japanese had the best fighter in the East. Their strikes used an excellent torpedo-bomber, the Nakajima B5N 'Kate' and the Japanese 'Stuka', the Aichi D3A 'Val' dive-bomber. Alone amongst the world's navies, the Japanese had developed in secret an oxygen-powered torpedo which, in its aerial version, could be successfully dropped from 1,000 feet. The Japanese pilots were veterans of the campaigns in China and Manchuria, some of them with a thousand flying hours, and great experience of horizontal and dive-bombing techniques. They had all trained long and hard for Pearl Harbor, exercising for months in the realistic conditions of the stormy North Pacific.

The Striking Force for Pearl Harbor, commanded by Vice-Admiral Chuichi Nagumo, consisted of the six carriers, two battleships, three cruisers and nine destroyers. This force, with a replenishment group of eight tankers and supply ships, sailed in secrecy from Tankan Bay in the Kurile Islands, north of Japan, on 26 November 1941, to begin its long and circuitous journey of some 3,000 miles to the flying-off position 200 miles north of Honolulu. The code-signal approving the attack, 'Niitaka Yama Nobore' ('Climb Mount

Above: Japanese Zero fighter taking off from *Akagi* to escort bombers striking at Pearl Harbor

Below: Vice-Admiral Chuichi Nagumo, commander of the Japanese Striking Force that attacked Pearl Harbor

Niitaka'), was received on board Nagumo's flagship *Akagi* on 1 December. The attack was fixed to begin at 8 a.m. Honolulu time, 7 December.

The strike was launched in two waves, the first beginning to take off at about 6 a.m. Led by the air group commander, Commander Mitsuo Fuchida, the first wave had fifty Kates armed with 1,760 lb armour-piercing bombs, another seventy Kates loaded with torpedoes fitted with special fins for shallow running, and fifty-one Vals loaded with 550 kg bombs. The fighter escort was forty-three Zekes who would also strafe ground positions once air superiority had been won.

It was a fine, calm Sunday morning when the first bombers arrived over Oahu shortly before eight o'clock. The islands seemed asleep in the early sunshine. The surprise was complete. Not a gun had fired, not a single fighter had taken off when simultaneously the torpedo-carrying Kates dived on Battleship Row and the Vals dived on rows of aircraft parked nearly wingtip to wingtip on the army airfield at Wheeler Field, at Ford Island in the middle of Pearl Harbor, and at airfields at Hickam, Ewa and the seaplane base at Kaneohe Bay. Zekes, sure of no opposition, flew in behind them to strafe anything that moved. No sooner had the first Vals lifted from their dropping runs than the high-level Kates arrived overhead to bomb Battleship Row, and cruisers and destroyers alongside and in dry dock.

The second wave, led by Lt.-Com. Shimazaki of *Zuikaku*, took off an hour later. It was another massive force of fifty-four Kates armed with 550 lb bombs, eighty Vals, and thirty-six Zekes as escort. This attack flew in on the opposite, eastern side of Oahu to bomb the airfields and the ships in harbour again. The Kates over Kaneohe and Hickam were

Above: A Japanese Kate flying over Wheeler Airfield during the attack on Pearl Harbor

Above left: A Kate torpedo-bomber taking off to strike Pearl Harbor. The Nakajima B5N2 saw service in China before the Second World War, and ended its war career as a suicide bomber in 1945. Engine: one 970 h.p. Nakajima Sakae 11 radial. Span: 50 ft. 11 in. Length: 33 ft. 9½ in. Maximum speed: 235 m.p.h. at 11,810 ft. Operational ceiling: 27,100 ft. Maximum range: 1,075 miles. Armament: two 7.7 mm. machine-guns in upper engine cowling and one or two in rear cockpit; one 1,764 lb. torpedo, or three 551 lb. bombs beneath the fuselage

Below left: Pearl Harbor hit by bombs and torpedoes: the battleship *California* sinks slowly into the mud while clouds of black oily smoke conceal all but the hulk of the capsized battleship *Oklahoma* (extreme right), 7 December 1941

unmolested but the Vals attacking the main harbour met much more determined flak opposition from the ships, which were now thoroughly roused. Nevertheless they hit some of the battleships which had been torpedoed in the first attack again and again with 550 lb bombs.

At about ten o'clock, everything went quiet. The Japanese aircraft flew away and returned jubilantly to their carriers, to the great relief of Nagumo, who had never shared Yamamoto's faith in a pre-emptive strike against a heavily defended target like Pearl Harbor.

Behind them, Nagumo's aircrews had left Battleship Row a burning, smoking shambles. *West Virginia* was sinking, *Arizona* had settled on the bottom, *Oklahoma* rolled over and capsized, and *California* was so badly damaged she eventually sank. *Nevada* had managed to get under way during the attack and was beached in the channel. The old target battleship *Utah* had sunk until only her upperworks could be seen. *Maryland*, *Pennsylvania* and *Tennessee* were all damaged. The cruisers *Raleigh*, *Helena* and *Honolulu*, the destroyers *Shaw*, *Cassin* and *Downes*, the repair ship *Vestal* and the seaplane tender *Curtiss* were also damaged. Ninety-two Navy and ninety-six Army aircraft had been destroyed and many others damaged. Casualties were 2,335 killed and 1,143 wounded. The Japanese had lost twenty-five aircraft, and all five of a force of midget submarines who had attacked and achieved nothing.

Fuchida and the other air group commanders pressed Nagumo to carry out another strike the next day. He refused, feeling that a second attack would be tempting fate. He ordered the force to break off and join the replenishment group. To the cautious Nagumo it must have seemed that Japan had achieved victory enough.

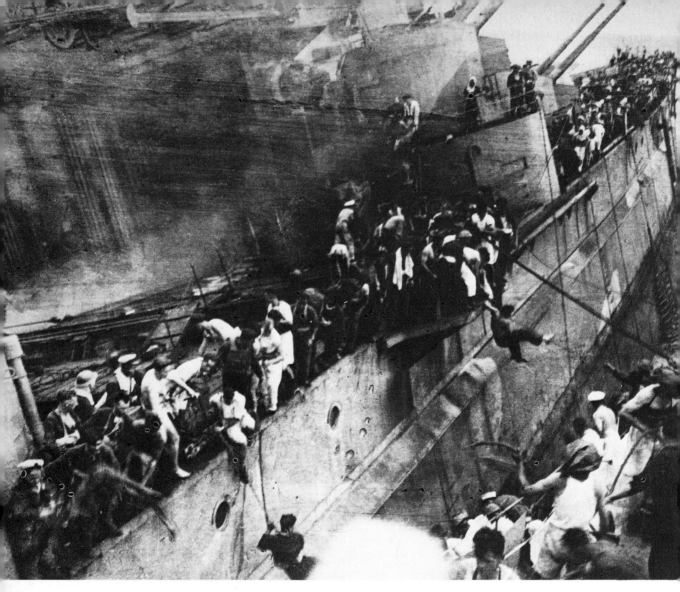

The destruction of Force Z: the battleship *Prince of Wales* sinking after air attack while the destroyer *Express* comes alongside to take off survivors, South China Sea, November 1941

So indeed it seemed, at the time. But Nagumo should have ordered a second strike. His aircrews would have found Pearl Harbor still in a state of shock and would also have had a good chance of destroying the two carriers *Enterprise* and *Lexington* who had both been absent the day before, delivering aircraft to Wake Island and Midway. Oil storage tanks which would have taken months to refill, and Pearl Harbor's great base and repair facilities had all been left untouched. In sinking those battleships the Japanese had demonstrated their irrelevance. The arbiters of the Pacific sea war would be airborne bombs and torpedoes. Unwittingly, the Imperial Japanese Navy had thrust the United States Navy into the aircraft carrier age. Shock, anger and a furious desire for vengeance united American public opinion behind the war as nothing else could have done, and so ensured the eventual defeat of Germany and of Japan. So, ironically, Pearl Harbor proved not to be a victory at all in the long run.

The last moments of Force Z: the battlecruiser *Repulse* (top) and the battleship *Prince of Wales* under attack by Japanese aircraft in the South China Sea, 10 December 1941

The destruction of Force Z

At the time, Pearl Harbor was a disaster for the U.S. Navy and it was followed three days later by another disaster inflicted on the Royal Navy. On 10 December 1941, the battleship *Prince of Wales* and the battlecruiser *Repulse* were both sunk in the South China Sea by Japanese aircraft of the 22nd Air Flotilla flying from bases near Saigon. This double blow was perhaps felt more deeply in the nation's core than any other the

The cruiser *Cornwall* sinking after she and her sister ship *Dorsetshire* had been caught and overwhelmed by a force of over fifty Japanese dive-bombers

country had suffered at sea. Churchill himself said that on hearing the news he never in all the war received a more direct shock. It was a severe strategic setback for the Allies, a shocking tactical defeat for the Navy, and a great personal tragedy for the officers and men of the ships involved.

The cause of the tragedy was, simply, lack of fighter cover at a critical time and place. But the reasons for that lack were complex and arose from a train of most unfortunate circumstances. As the situation in the Far East deteriorated, Churchill had pressed for a modern capital ship to be sent out to act as a deterrent and a threat to the Japanese, exactly as *Tirpitz* was already doing for the Allies in northern waters. The Admiralty demurred, not wishing to send capital ships into such an exposed position, but under strong pressure from Churchill and from the Foreign Secretary Anthony Eden, Force Z, consisting of *Prince of Wales*, *Repulse* and four destroyers, had assembled at Singapore by the beginning of December. Force Z was commanded by Admiral Sir Tom Phillips, who had been Vice-Chief of Naval Staff for much of the war. Admiral Phillips firmly believed in the ability of anti-aircraft guns to put up a wall of steel to protect his ships against air attack. He also discounted the danger that the Japanese might be able to mount air attacks at much greater ranges than the Royal Navy. The new aircraft carrier *Indomitable* should have accompanied Force Z but she had been damaged by an accidental grounding at Kingston, Jamaica, whilst working up in November. Thus everything seemed to conspire to make Force Z vulnerable to air attack.

Simultaneously with their attack at Pearl Harbor, the Japanese also attacked Guam, Wake Island, Hong Kong, the Philippines and Malaya. On 6 December a Japanese invasion force was reported approaching the Malayan peninsula from Indochina. The Japanese landed at Khota Baru in northern Malaya and at Singora in Thailand on the

The cruisers *Dorsetshire* and
Cornwall undergoing the dive-
bombing attacks which eventually
sank them both, Indian Ocean,
5 April 1942

7th and 8th. Perhaps, in view of what was about to happen, it would have been better if Force Z had then sailed and disappeared into the maze of islands of Indonesia, as was suggested, to exert a vague threat on Japanese planning and movements. But having arrived at Singapore, and having been seen and acclaimed by the population, it was unthinkable for Admiral Phillips to do nothing when the enemy were actually invading. He decided that if two essential requirements, surprise and adequate fighter cover off Singora, could both be fulfilled, his force stood an excellent chance of destroying the invasion force and disrupting the Japanese communications. Force Z therefore sailed from Singapore on the evening of the 8th, and steamed north.

Early on 9 December Admiral Phillips had a signal from Singapore telling him that the fighter escort he had asked for could not be provided. Singapore's only fighters were a small force of obsolescent Brewster Buffaloes, and in any case the forward air-strips at Khota Baru had already been overrun by the enemy. That afternoon a Japanese reconnaissance plane was sighted to the north. It had to be assumed that Force Z had been discovered. With no fighter cover, and all surprise gone, Admiral Phillips had no choice but to abandon the operation. Force Z steamed on northwards until after dark, to confuse the enemy, and then turned back towards Singapore. Ironically, had Force Z steamed north just a little further they would have sighted four Japanese cruisers within range of their guns. The reconnaissance aircraft had come from these cruisers and had not reported Force Z to Saigon.

However, Force Z had already been reported to Saigon by the submarine I.65 who had sighted them that afternoon. At the time Admiral Sadaichi Matsunaga's 22nd Air Flotilla were preparing to fly off a bombing strike against *Prince of Wales* and *Repulse* who had been reported still alongside in Singapore that morning. The 22nd Air Flotilla was the

Japanese equivalent of Fliegerkorps X. They had trained for some time for their anti-shipping role. Their three divisions, the Mihoro, the Genzan and the Kanoya, were equipped with ninety-six Betty bombers and forty-eight Nell bombers, all with an operational range of 1,500 miles and capable of carrying either bombs or the Mark 91 naval torpedo.

The bombers were hastily rearmed with torpedoes and had taken off by 7 p.m. that evening. The chances of sighting the enemy by night were slim, and they might even be confused with their own ships, but the risk to the landing force was so great that Admiral Matsunaga could not afford to take chances. However, the strike saw nothing and returned disappointed, with their torpedoes still on board.

Meanwhile Admiral Phillips had received another signal informing him of yet another Japanese landing, at Kuantan. The signal was unauthenticated, but Kuantan was further south, only a short detour off Force Z's homeward route. Admiral Phillips decided to investigate, but did not signal his intention. Radio silence was all-important. He must have believed that the staff in Singapore would assume that he would go to Kuantan and would know that he would obviously need fighter cover off the coast there at first light. A brilliant staff officer himself, Admiral Phillips evidently expected (vainly, as it turned out) the same degree of almost telepathic flair in others.

At 2.20 a.m. on the morning of the 10th, Force Z was sighted again by the submarine I.58 who found herself in the path of the oncoming heavy ships. I.58 dived and fired a salvo of five torpedoes, which missed, and then surfaced again to send off her report that Force Z was now steaming south.

In Saigon the last planes from the night strike had only landed on at 2.30 a.m., but by 6 a.m. the first of a new strike were on their way. Three 'Babs' and nine Bettys of the Genzan Corps flew off on a sector search and were soon followed by thirty-four Nells with bombs and twenty-six Nells and twenty-six Bettys armed with torpedoes.

By 8 a.m. that morning, Force Z was off Kuantan. The signal had clearly been false. There was some small shipping about, which Admiral Phillips decided to investigate, but no sign of an invasion.

The searching aircraft of the Japanese strike had passed Force Z without spotting them. Some of the attackers had flown well south of the latitude of Singapore. There had been some brief excitement at about 10 a.m. when some of the Genzan Corps fell upon the destroyer *Tenedos*, who was making her way to Singapore independently of Force Z. *Tenedos* evaded all the bombs and signalled that she was under air attack.

Tenedos's signal was the first indication Admiral Phillips had that his force was in any danger. In fact, the danger was imminent. The Japanese aircraft had been in the air for five hours. Most of them were flying northwards, disappointed at having missed their targets. At 11.05 a.m. Ensign Hoashi in a Babs reconnaissance aircraft sighted two heavy ships through a break in clouds and broadcast a general call. Now that they had a bearing, the strike pressed forward. Lt. Sadao Takai in the Genzan Corps wrote, when the enemy fleet was expected to be sighted at any moment, 'I became nervous, and shaky and could not dismiss the sensation. I had the strongest urge to urinate. It was exactly like the sensation one feels before entering a contest in an athletic meeting.'[12]

The Japanese flying was of a very high standard. The first high-level bombers scored several near misses, and one direct hit on *Repulse* amidships at 11.13 a.m. The torpedo-bombers were to make their runs simultaneously to distract the defences, but they were late. However, they hit *Prince of Wales* with two torpedoes, damaging her propellers and steering gear. Perhaps her wireless aerials were also damaged, because Admiral Phillips seemed to keep radio silence to the end. After the action had lasted nearly an hour, Captain Tennant in *Repulse* was appalled to find that no signal had been made to Singapore; on his own initiative he signalled that the force was under air attack. In the meantime there were so many aircraft attacking, so many torpedoes streaking through the water from both sides at once, that *Repulse* could not avoid them all. At 12.20 she had her first hit, and four minutes later sustained four more torpedo hits. The ship hung at an angle of sixty or seventy degrees to port for several minutes and then, at 12.33, she finally sank.

The flagship was some way off to the south, also under constant bomb and torpedo attack. The two capital ships and their destroyer escorts had put up the expected steel barrage, but it was not enough. *Prince of Wales* bore another three hits which brought her almost to a standstill. At 1.05 p.m. the destroyer *Express* came alongside the starboard quarter to take off wounded and men not essential for the fighting. It was almost too late. *Prince of Wales* was finished, and at 1.20 she also sank. Overhead, Ensign Hoashi was still giving a running commentary to his colleagues and to Saigon of the destruction of the battleship. The Buffaloes from Singapore arrived in time to fly over the scene of floating debris and giant oil slicks, in which the destroyers were circling to pick up survivors. 840 officers and men of Force **Z** were lost, including Admiral Phillips and Captain John Leach, of *Prince of Wales*.

The destruction of Force **Z** drew the final curtains over the battleship era. It was also to be the first time for hundreds of years that the Royal Navy lost its supremacy in any theatre of a war at sea and failed eventually to regain it. From that day, the U.S. Navy assumed the mantle in the Far East and when the Royal Navy again appeared in strength it was very much as the junior partner.

Raid in the Indian Ocean

The only naval ships left to dispute the Far East with the Japanese were a mixed British, Australian, Dutch and American force of cruisers and destroyers who were very badly mauled in the forlorn battles of the Java Sea in February and March 1942. After the fall of Singapore the base of the Eastern Fleet was moved to Colombo where, in March 1942, Admiral Sir James Somerville arrived to take over as C.-in-C.

As Yamamoto had prophesied, Nagumo's Striking Force was able to range unchecked through the length and breadth of eastern waters, striking at Rabaul, at Amboina in New Guinea, at Darwin in Northern Australia, bombing and strafing the town and sinking shipping in the harbour, and at Tjilatjap in Java before, on 26 March, heading westwards across the Indian Ocean.

The Eastern Fleet had a reasonable strength, on paper. But four of Somerville's battleships were the slow and obsolete 'R' Class. One of his three carriers was *Hermes*, and the aircrews of the two modern ships *Formidable* and *Indomitable* needed more experience before taking on the Japanese. Nevertheless Somerville had his fleet at sea by 1 April, waiting for the Japanese. But by the time they were located fuel shortage had forced the fleet to retire to Addu Atoll and the Japanese appeared at a very awkward time, when Somerville's newer and faster ships were refuelling. Somerville put to sea again, hoping for a shot at the enemy, perhaps with a night torpedo

The aircraft carrier *Hermes* sinking off the coast of Ceylon after a deadly Japanese air attack had inflicted ten bomb hits in forty minutes, 9 April 1942

A barrel sprouting wings appears,
Its Cyclone cowl a letter "O,"
No double X for strength it bears,
Superfluous in Buffalo.

attack by his Albacores. The chance never came. Perhaps it was as well. Although the Eastern Fleet were disappointed by the lack of action, the raiders included five of the six carriers that had struck Pearl Harbor and an engagement with them might well have been another disaster for the Royal Navy.

Nagumo's aircrews snapped up the crumbs left for them. On Easter Sunday, 5 April, they attacked Colombo with ninety-one bombers and thirty fighters. The harbour had been cleared and the strike did nothing like as much damage as at Darwin. But that afternoon the Japanese chanced on the cruisers *Dorsetshire* and *Cornwall*, on their way to rejoin the fleet. They were overwhelmed by a force of over fifty dive-bombers and were both sunk.

Whilst all the time keeping a sharp eye on the lookout for Somerville's main fleet, Nagumo attacked Trincomalee on 9 April. This harbour had also been cleared of shipping, including *Hermes*, the destroyer *Vampire* and the corvette *Hollyhock*. Unluckily, these three were discovered, hugging the coast of Ceylon, and the Japanese aircrews swung into their usual deadly action. All three ships were sunk, *Hermes* after sustaining ten direct bomb hits in forty minutes. In the north, meanwhile, Vice-Admiral Ozawa, with one light carrier, cruisers and destroyers, was sinking twenty merchant ships and otherwise doing much as he pleased off Vizagapatam.

'Victory Disease'

When Nagumo retired from the Indian Ocean and returned to Japan on 18 April he and his aircrews were given a hero's welcome. Naval air power had enabled Japan to inflict numbing blows upon the world's two largest and strongest navies and to strike at will across one third of the earth's surface, from Wake Island to Colombo. It was no wonder that, by their own admission, the Japanese were suffering from 'Victory Disease'. It was an affliction which the Greeks called *hubris*. It was almost always followed by *nemesis*.

By mid-May 1942 the last American garrisons in the Philippines, on the peninsula of Bataan and the island of Corregidor, had surrendered. The British and Indian armies were reaching the Assam border, after a retreat of 1,000 miles, the longest in their military history. In six months Japan had conquered an empire of 90 million people which stretched from Rabaul to Rangoon and which contained the rich oil of Indonesia and Borneo, 88 per cent of the world's rubber, 54 per cent of its tin, 30 per cent of its rice and 20 per cent of its tungsten. In so doing they had lost about 15,000 men, about 400 aircraft, and twenty-three warships, none of them bigger than a destroyer.

5
Turning Point in the East

Now, when the whole Orient resounded with their victories, when they really did seem invincible, at sea, in the air and in the jungle, the Japanese over-reached themselves. Having achieved their war objectives so quickly and economically, they could now reinforce their success in Burma and attack in China, as the Army Staff wished. They could press down the island chain of New Guinea and the Solomons to Port Moresby and Guadalcanal to isolate Australia from Japan's conquests, as the Navy Staff preferred. Or they could fulfil Admiral Yamamoto's great dream of one decisive encounter with the U.S. Fleet, to finish off the task left over from Pearl Harbor. General Doolittle's raid in April 1942, when B-25 Mitchell bombers took off from the carrier *Hornet* and cheekily bombed Tokyo and other cities, seemed to reinforce Yamamoto's opinion; the physical damage was small, but the blow to Japanese pride was great. In the event, the Japanese undertook the drive towards Port Moresby *and* the confrontation with the U.S. fleet, which proved too much for their resources.

The Japanese could have assembled an invasion force, given it as strong an escort as possible, and simply sent it to Port Moresby. But that was not their way. Whenever they had enough ships the Japanese over-elaborated. They split their force into separate groups, with separate objectives. They laid intricate traps, involving complicated diversions, decoys and pincer movements. Japanese plans required a

Dauntless dive-bombers and Wildcat fighters (forward) ranged on the flight deck of U.S.S. *Enterprise*

59

Opposite: Admiral Chester W. Nimitz

degree of cooperation between ships which no navy in the world has ever achieved. They made few allowances for contingencies. Most dangerous of all, they relied on the enemy doing what was expected of him.

Battle of the Coral Sea

Task Force Mo, formed to capture Port Moresby, consisted of an invasion group of eleven transports escorted by destroyers, which was to sail from Rabaul on 4 May 1942. A smaller group was to invade Tulagi in the Solomon Islands and set up a seaplane base there. A support group including a seaplane carrier was to establish a similar base in the Louisades. The main covering group under Rear-Admiral Aritome Goto, with the light carrier *Shoho*, four heavy cruisers and a destroyer, was to cover the Tulagi landing and then double back and do the same at Port Moresby. A striking force with *Zuikaku* and *Shokaku* under Vice-Admiral Takagi was to sail from Truk down the northern side of the Solomons and round San Cristobal, to enter the Coral Sea from the east. Admiral Shigeyoshi Inouye, who commanded ashore in Rabaul, intended that any American force which tried to molest the Port Moresby landing would be caught between the pincers

Below: The Doolittle Raid, 18 April 1942: B-25 Mitchell bombers warming up on the flight deck of *Hornet* en route to bomb Tokyo

of Goto and Takagi. Once the Allied force had been destroyed the Japanese would control the Coral Sea and could go on to bomb and neutralize air bases in Queensland and invade the Ocean and Nauru Islands, with their phosphates, essential to Japanese agriculture. It was an ambitious but an ingenious plan. But for the weather and Japanese mistakes it might have worked.

Port Moresby, at the tip of Papua commanding the Coral Sea and the southern approaches to Australia, was vital to the Allies, not only for the protection of Australia but as a launching point for future offensives. It had to be defended, and the Allies' defence was greatly helped by the breaking of the secret Japanese 'purple' naval codes. By the end of April 1942 Admiral Chester Nimitz, C.-in-C. Pacific, had concluded that the Japanese's next objective was Port Moresby, and the target date probably early in May.

It was one thing to know the enemy's intentions, and quite another to defeat them. There were some 300 U.S.A.A.F. and R.A.A.F. land-based aircraft available for search and long-range attacks, but they were in General MacArthur's South-West Pacific Command. The Combined Chiefs of Staff had already approved strict demarcation rules between the two commands. Unlike Inouye, who would have the 25th Air Flotilla under his hand at Rabaul, Nimitz would have to rely on what cooperation he could get from MacArthur, whose aircrews were in any case inexperienced at identifying and attacking shipping.

Clearly Nimitz would have to rely on his own air power. He formed his ships into two groups, Task Force 17 centred on the carrier *Yorktown* and commanded by Rear-Admiral Frank Fletcher, and Task Force 11, with the carrier *Lexington*, under Rear-Admiral Aubrey W. Fitch. They were joined by Task Force 44, commanded by Rear-Admiral J. C. Crace R.N., with the two heavy cruisers *Australia* and *Hobart*. Nimitz also had some battleships, but it was already clear to him that they were only auxiliaries in the Pacific battles to come, and he kept them on the west coast of America. Nimitz gave overall command to Fletcher, who was dispatched to operate in the Coral Sea; how, when and where was left to Fletcher. This marvellous reliance on the man on the spot contrasted strongly with some of the Royal Navy's unfortunate experiences of interference from home.

Fletcher's force mustered 141 aircraft. The fleet fighter was the Grumman F4F Wildcat, known to the R.N. as the Martlet. The dive-bombers were Douglas SBD-III Dauntlesses, and the torpedo-bombers, Douglas TBD-1 Devastators. Both these last types were obsolescent but still in squadron service. *Yorktown* was a new carrier, completed in 1938.

Above: 'Lady Lex', U.S.S. *Lexington:* probably the last photograph of this much-loved ship in an operational state before she was attacked during the Battle of the Coral Sea, 8 May 1942, and had to be sunk

Lexington was a veteran, completed in 1927, but extensively modernized since. The aircrews were among the most experienced in the U.S.N.; some of *Lexington's* ship's company had served in her since she first commissioned.

Fletcher's two groups met in the Coral Sea on 1 May, about 250 miles south-west of Espiritu Santo, and began refuelling. The next day Fletcher left Fitch to finish fuelling and jauntily set off himself westwards to look for the Japanese. He thus split his force in the likely presence of an enemy. Had Takagi been nearer, Fletcher might have been made to pay for his *insouciance*.

On the evening of the 3rd Fletcher heard of the Japanese landing at Tulagi and steamed north to launch three strikes of Dauntlesses and Devastators on 4 May. Vast amounts of bombs, torpedoes and ammunition were expended to achieve what Nimitz later called 'disappointing results'. Fletcher's aircrews greatly over-estimated their successes, however, and

Below: Lexington after two torpedo and two bomb hits. Everything seemed under control until a petrol explosion caused by a spark from a generator. *Lexington* later had to be abandoned and sunk by a destroyer's torpedo

Task Force 17 returned in very good heart to meet Fitch and Crace the next day and, once more, refuel.

That same day Takagi entered the Coral Sea from the north, and he was actually only about seventy miles to the north of Fletcher early on the morning of 6 May. Fletcher's ships were then out in the open, in clear, brilliant sunshine. But amazingly, Takagi's carrier admiral, Rear-Admiral Tadaichi Hara, had ordered no searches to be flown to the south-east, while Fletcher's search aircraft stopped short of Takagi, who was then under thick cloud overcast. So neither side had definite knowledge of the other and a good chance for a carrier battle, on terms favourable to Takagi, passed him by. After fuelling, the tanker *Neosho* with her escorting destroyer *Sims* were detached to steam southwards to the next fuelling rendezvous.

Action began at last on 7 May. Inexplicably, Fletcher sent Crace westwards to attack the Port Moresby Invasion Group, thereby weakening his own screen and also depriving part of his force of air protection. Crace's ships were duly attacked by aircraft from Rabaul and, incidentally, by aircraft of the U.S.A.A.F. Having withstood an air attack as strong as that which had sunk *Prince of Wales* and *Repulse*, Crace broke off to the south when, some time later, he heard that the invasion force had retired.

Meanwhile one of Hara's reconnaissance aircraft reported a carrier and a cruiser to the south and Hara at once launched a bomb and torpedo strike at maximum strength. In fact, the 'carrier and the cruiser' were *Neosho* and *Sims*. Hara had committed his main force to a minor target. *Sims* was sunk, *Neosho* was badly damaged and drifted for four days before being scuttled.

Fletcher had been lucky. *Neosho* and *Sims* had drawn off Hara's main assault, while Crace had diverted the main land-based attack from Rabaul. When one of his searchers reported 'two carriers and four heavy cruisers' Fletcher launched a strike of some ninety aircraft from the two carriers, without waiting to verify the targets. When the scout returned it was found that through a decoding error the message should have read 'two heavy cruisers and two destroyers'. So Fletcher, too, had committed his main force to an unknown target. Bravely, he allowed the strike to proceed and once again he was lucky. *Lexington*'s attackers, flying ahead of *Yorktown*'s, sighted an aircraft carrier with an escort about twenty-five miles to starboard of their course. They turned aside and found *Shoho*. The two carriers' air groups over-powered *Shoho* with thirteen bomb and seven torpedo hits. She sank at 11.33 a.m. and the listeners in the operations rooms heard Lt.-Com. R. E. Dixon, leading one of *Lexington*'s

Above: The Japanese aircraft carrier *Shoho* torpedoed and later sunk during the Battle of the Coral Sea

Below: Vice-Admiral Frank J. Fletcher who commanded the U.S. Fleet in the Battle of the Coral Sea

Dauntless squadrons, call out loud and clear, 'Scratch one flattop! Dixon to Carrier, Scratch one flattop!'

Lexington and *Yorktown* were ready to launch a second strike in the afternoon, but Fletcher decided against it, still not knowing where the two big carriers were. The initiative passed temporarily to Takagi. So far the battle had been a series of humiliating mischances and blunders for Takagi and Hara. But their aircrews were still supremely confident, and there was still a chance to retrieve the day. A strike was launched at Fletcher at 4.30 p.m. (7 May) in poor visibility and thick cloud. The attackers missed Fletcher's ships and lost nine aircraft shot down by intercepting Wildcats. Worse still, several others mistook *Yorktown* for *Shokaku* in the overcast and tried to land on. One was shot down. With more losses while trying to find and land on their own carriers, all but six of the twenty-seven in that strike were lost.

During that night, both fleet commanders considered and rejected plans for a surface night action. The main battle therefore took place on 8 May, with strike and counter-strike between carriers. Fletcher's ships were now well into the Coral Sea, in exactly the position the Japanese had hoped. But the famous 'pincer' had lost its power. *Shoho* was gone, and Hara's air groups had suffered losses. Both sides were able to muster about 120 aircraft, but the balance of experience still lay in favour of the Japanese. The invasion force had been ordered by the timid Inouye to withdraw, but it was still quite possible for Hara to redress the situation and for the invasion to go ahead.

Both sides launched searches before dawn and sighted each other at about the same time, although Hara had gained time by launching his strike without waiting for a precise sighting report. But the Americans were the first to attack, arriving over *Shokaku* and *Zuikaku* shortly before 11 a.m. *Zuikaku*

Douglas SBD Dauntlesses attacking the Japanese Fleet, Midway, June 1942.

was hidden by clouds and the main attack fell upon *Shokaku*. The torpedoes missed but three bomb hits set *Shokaku* on fire forward, so that she could recover but not launch aircraft. She was detached to Truk and, though she nearly capsized on the way, eventually reached Japan.

The American attack had been badly coordinated and over twenty of the bombers failed to find the enemy at all. Not so the Japanese. *Lexington* and *Yorktown* were in brilliant sunshine, with visibility almost unlimited, when Hara's aircrews went into action with all their old panache. Eighteen torpedo-bombers, thirty-three bombers and eighteen fighters attacked the American carriers at about the same time as the Americans were delivering their own attacks. Both carriers were hit, *Yorktown* by one bomb forward which did no

The fuselage is short and fat,
The plank-like wings are square and
    flat,
While out behind in foul or fair,
The Martlet's tail stands fair and
    square.

serious damage, *Lexington* by two torpedoes and two bombs. So often in the Pacific carriers survived the initial damage only to be lost later by petrol fires and explosions: in *Lexington* the first fires were put out, the list taken off the ship by counter-flooding and everything seemed under control when, at 12.47 p.m., there was a petrol explosion caused by a spark from a generator. Soon there was a second explosion, fierce fires were raging, and at 5.10 that evening *Lexington* had to be abandoned. At 8 p.m. a destroyer sank her with one torpedo.

Yamamoto ordered Takagi to return, but Fletcher had withdrawn. The battle was over. If the Port Moresby invasion group had turned back then they would have stood a good chance of success. They would only have been opposed by land-based aircraft who were demonstrably not good at attacking ships. But this is to be wise after the event.

So ended the Battle of the Coral Sea, the first in naval history fought entirely between carriers, when at no time did any ship on either side sight an opponent. Tactically, it was yet another Japanese victory. *Shoho* was a very fair exchange for *Sims*, *Neosho* and the valuable and much-loved 'Lady Lex'. However, *Shokaku* was very badly damaged and *Zuikaku*'s air group had suffered losses; both carriers needed time to repair and retrain and so neither was present at the coming battle of Midway, when either or both might have tipped the scales in Japan's favour.

Strategically, the Coral Sea action was an Allied victory. Japanese invasion plans had received a very severe reverse. And the moral effect was enormous. The Japanese aircraft carriers were not invincible after all!

Midway

On 5 May 1942, while the battle in the Coral Sea was still in progress, Admiral Yamamoto had received from Imperial Japanese Headquarters a directive to carry out Operation MI, which was the invasion and occupation of Midway Island and the Western Aleutians, the target date for invasion of Midway being the night of 5/6 June. The seizure of Midway would give the Japanese the invaluable strategic prize of an advanced warning and defence post at the western end of the Hawaiian chain. More important to Yamamoto, a move against Midway was bound to bring about a confrontation with the U.S. Fleet.

Yamamoto's desire for one decisive battle was strategically sound, but it was ironic that at the very time he could have achieved his dearest wish he chose to disperse his forces to pursue different objectives, thus risking defeat in detail. The very success of their aircraft carriers led the Japanese to neglect ordinary rules of naval warfare. Yamamoto could have

The Japanese aircraft carrier *Hiryu* attacked and sinking off Midway, June 1942; the last photograph of her, taken from a Japanese aircraft

drawn up his vast armada of eight aircraft carriers with their 400 aircraft, eleven battleships, thirteen heavy cruisers, eleven light cruisers and over sixty destroyers, and simply advanced on Midway. The American fleet had to give battle, as indeed they did, and Yamamoto's strength should have been more than enough to overpower them.

Instead, Yamamoto prepared a typically Japanese plan, involving no less than five major forces, some of which were themselves further divided into two, three or four subdivisions. An Advance Expeditionary Force of submarines was flung out in a line to report on the American fleet movements when, as Yamamoto expected, it sallied forth from Pearl Harbor as Midway came under attack. The Carrier Striking Force, commanded by Nagumo, flying his flag in *Akagi*, with *Kaga*, *Hiryu* and *Soryu*, would strike first at Midway, and then at the expected American fleet when it arrived. The Midway Occupation Force, under Vice-Admiral Nobutake Kondo, had battleships, heavy cruisers, transports, seaplane tenders and minesweepers. Admiral Yamamoto himself commanded the main body, which had three battleships, one of them the 60,000 ton, 18-inch gun monster *Yamato*. A Northern Area Force, with its own carriers and cruisers under Vice-Admiral Boshiro Hosogaya, would attack the Aleutian islands of Adak Attu and Kiska. This, Yamamoto hoped, would at the least distract attention and at best divert powerful American forces northwards.

The plan was for Nagumo's carriers to strike Midway and then, if the American fleet came out, Yamamoto's main body would move up. The Allies would be crushed in the triple pincers of Nagumo's carriers, Yamamoto's battleships, and the battleships of Kondo's Midway Occupation Force.

It was odd that Yamamoto, the great architect of carrier warfare, should still yearn to destroy his enemy by heavy guns. His battleships would have been far better employed in close support of the carriers. If they had been, the battle might have gone differently.

Yamamoto's other error was excusable. Not aware that Japanese codes had been broken, he believed that the American fleet would not leave Pearl Harbor until the first news that Midway was under attack. Aircrew reports from the Coral Sea suggested that both American carriers were too badly damaged to take part, even if the fleet did put to sea. In short, the Japanese acted on the belief that it was virtually impossible for opposing carriers to be anywhere near Midway when it was attacked.

In fact, Nimitz already knew in remarkable detail of Yamamoto's intentions, his targets and his likeliest dates. The Japanese submarines, though late on their stations, saw nothing. The American fleet was well past them before they arrived.

Pearl Harbor dockyard, working day and night, repaired *Yorktown*'s battle damage in two days (Fitch had reckoned on a minimum of ninety) and she was able to sail with the rest of the fleet on 31 May. Nimitz had at his disposal three carriers with a total of 230 aircraft, thirteen cruisers and about thirty destroyers. He still had his battleships and still deployed them off the west coast. On Midway Island there was a heterogeneous collection of about 150 aircraft, from B-17 Flying Fortresses to Buffaloes, and including six of the new Grumman Avenger TBRs which were to replace the Devastator.

Nimitz once again divided his force into two groups. Task Force 16, centred on the carriers *Enterprise* and *Hornet*, should have been commanded by Rear-Admiral Halsey. Because of an irritating skin disease Halsey was replaced for the operation by Rear-Admiral Raymond Spruance, who was to emerge as the greatest sea captain of the Pacific. Task Force 17, with *Yorktown*, was commanded by Admiral Fletcher, who was also in overall command.

Nimitz ordered Fletcher to take station north-east of Midway, where long-range 700-mile searches from the island could detect the Japanese fleet, while his own carriers still lay undetected. He also sent five cruisers and thirteen destroyers north to engage the Aleutian attack force.

The components of Yamamoto's great fleet sailed from several ports, in Japan and the Marianas, at the end of May. By 1 June they were heading east through fog, rain, and high winds. On 3 and 4 June aircraft from the carriers *Ryujo* and *Junyo* attacked Dutch Harbour in the Aleutians. The islands were lightly defended and the Japanese eventually occupied them, after some minor naval engagements. But Nimitz was not to be drawn into this sideshow. He knew that the vital battle would be fought around Midway and this opened, also on 3 June, with the sighting by a Catalina 700 miles west of Midway of some tankers and storeships of the Midway Occupation Force. The pilot excitably reported them as battleships and aircraft carriers. Aircraft from Midway attacked, but hit only one ship. Shore-based aircraft had very little effect in the battle, although they did at one time create a crucial diversion.

Nimitz and Fletcher knew from decoded signals that this could not be their main opponent. Nagumo's carriers were much closer, probably not more than 400 miles west of Midway. That night Fletcher and Spruance steamed south-west to close the distance. Nagumo, although ignorant of Fletcher and Spruance, also steamed to close, to launch his

A Japanese Kate torpedo-bomber takes off from a Japanese aircraft carrier at Midway

Midway strike at dawn. Hence the main battle was to take place on 4 June.

By 4.30 a.m. both sides had flown off aircraft, Fletcher ten search Devastators, Nagumo his Midway strike of thirty-six Kates, thirty-six Vals, escorted by thirty-six Zekes, led by Lt. Tomonaga, of *Hiryu*. At 6.39 they were over Midway, strafing installations and oil tanks, destroying grounded aircraft, but failing to put the runways out of action. Overhead, the antique defending Buffaloes were outnumbered and badly mauled.

Forewarned by radar, Midway had already sent off a very mixed force of Flying Fortresses, new Avengers and ancient Vindicators to attack Nagumo. They achieved nothing, and sustained heavy losses, but they did distract Nagumo at a crucial time. He had just heard from Tomonaga that Midway needed another strike. These attacks seemed to confirm it. Nagumo had been keeping back a second force of ninety-three aircraft, armed with bombs and torpedoes, ready in case of interference by the American fleet. At 7.15 he ordered these aircraft struck down, to be rearmed with bombs for another strike at Midway. This was a fatal decision.

For once, Nagumo had been poorly served by his reconnaissance aircraft. His cruisers had begun flying off their search float-planes from 4.35 a.m., but the plane from *Tone* was delayed because of a catapult defect and did not take off until 5 a.m. Unluckily for the Japanese, the American fleet happened to lie in this delayed aircraft's search sector. At 7.28 the pilot sighted American ships and reported them. He did not mention carriers. Ships without carriers 200 miles away did not worry Nagumo, but he evidently had misgivings. At 7.45 he changed his mind and ordered those aircraft with bombs not yet unloaded to hold. Two minutes later he signalled to this maddeningly deliberate pilot to 'ascertain ship types'. To Nagumo's relief, the man reported, at 8.09, five cruisers and five destroyers. But, at 8.20, there came the dreaded message, 'Enemy ships appear to be accompanied by a carrier'.

Nagumo was in an agony of indecision. The report had come at the worst possible time. Some of his aircraft were in the hangars, some were still on deck, some were being unloaded with bombs and loaded with torpedoes, some were being refuelled. The returning strike from Midway had to be landed on. Rear-Admiral Yamaguchi in *Hiryu* suggested that his strike be flown off. Nagumo rejected the advice. He ordered all aircraft to be struck down, and the returning aircraft landed on. His defensive patrols were engaged in fighting off the Midway attackers and if he had launched a strike it would have had no fighter escort. In the middle of it all, the U.S. submarine *Nautilus* added to the confusion by carrying out a torpedo attack on a battleship.

Nagumo's Midway strike aircraft were landed on by 9.18 and at once all four carriers began furiously to rearm, refuel and range up a full strike against the American carriers.

Fletcher had paused to recover his search aircraft, and had ordered Spruance to go ahead to the south-west. Spruance had coldly calculated the best time to deliver his attack. He decided to time it so that he would catch Nagumo as he was recovering his Midway strike. He also decided to use every available aircraft, even if it meant that the first off had to orbit for an hour or more while a second group was ranged up and launched. The enemy had been reported 200 miles west-south-west of *Yorktown*.

At 7.02 the first of TF 16's strike of sixty-seven Dauntless dive-bombers, twenty-nine Devastator torpedo-bombers and twenty Wildcats took off. But the strike was not to be the combined blow intended. *Enterprise*'s Dauntlesses, led by

The carrier *Yorktown* crippled after three bomb and two torpedo hits; abandoned and sinking

Lt.-Com. McClusky, were ordered to go on, because the Task Force had been sighted by the Japanese, without waiting for the rest, and they took departure at 7.52. *Enterprise*'s fighters mistakenly took station above *Hornet*'s Devastators, leaving their own Devastators unescorted, while *Hornet*'s fighters lost their Devastators and flew with their bombers instead. So the strike flew in four separate groups: *Enterprise*'s dive-bombers, *Hornet*'s dive-bombers and the fighters, followed by the two torpedo-bomber squadrons.

While ranging up his next strike, Nagumo had steamed north-east, to close the distance. When TF 16's aircraft arrived at his reported position, the sea was empty. *Hornet*'s dive-bombers and fighters turned south-east and found nothing: the dive-bombers returned to *Hornet* or to Midway; the fighters ran out of fuel and ditched. The two torpedo-bomber squadrons turned north and just after 9.30 saw the Japanese carriers. With no fighter escort, skimming low over the sea, the Devastators were sitting ducks. Both squadron leaders, Waldron of *Hornet* and Lindsey of *Enterprise*, had known beforehand how vulnerable they were likely to be. Waldron had written: 'My greatest hope is that we encounter a favourable tactical situation, but if we don't, and the worst comes to the worst, I want each of us to do his utmost to destroy our enemies. If there is only one plane left to make a final run in, I want that man to go in and get a hit. May God be with us all.'[13]

Douglas SBD Dauntlesses over Midway Island. First entering service in November 1940, the Dauntless was the U.S. Navy's standard carrier-borne dive-bomber at Pearl Harbor and at Midway. A very robust aircraft, able to absorb great punishment, the Dauntless was later used from CVEs flying anti-submarine or close-support sorties. Engine: one 1,200 h.p. Wright R-1820-60 Cyclone radial. Span: 41 ft. 6 in. Length: 33 ft. Maximum speed: 252 m.p.h. at 13,800 ft. Operational ceiling: 24,300 ft. Range with 1,000 lb. bomb, 1,115 miles. Armament: two 0.50 in. machine-guns in front of fuselage, two 0.303 in. machine-guns in rear cockpit; one 1,000 lb. or 500 lb. bomb beneath fuselage, or two 100 lb. bombs or two 250 lb. depth-charges beneath the wings

The worst did come to the worst. The Devastators were no match for the Zekes, who wreaked a terrible slaughter. All Waldron's aircraft were shot down and only one man, Ensign Gay, survived by clinging to a rubber seat cushion and ducking underwater when strafing Zekes passed overhead. Ten of Lindsey's fourteen Devastators were also shot down. No torpedo hits were scored on any ship.

The Devastators' sacrifice had not been in vain. While the Zekes were attracted down to sea-level, the dive-bombers from *Enterprise* and from *Yorktown*, who had flown off an hour later, met over the Japanese fleet.

The timing was perfect. The Japanese rearming and ranging were complete. The flight decks were crowded with aircraft ready to take off and the carriers were racing up into the wind when the dive-bombers struck.

Akagi was hit once abreast the bridge and again aft amongst a crowd of aircraft. The fires, fed by petrol and spread by internal explosions of bombs and torpedoes, forced Nagumo to shift his flag to a cruiser. *Kaga* was hit four times, with the same fatal sequence of fires and explosions. *Soryu* was also hit three times and within twenty minutes was being abandoned. *Akagi* floated until that afternoon, when she was abandoned and sunk by a torpedo from a destroyer. *Kaga* had been abandoned earlier and broke in two after enormous internal explosions that evening. *Soryu*, also a mass of flames and smoke, sank at about the same time.

Only *Hiryu*, some distance ahead of the others, escaped, and at noon her aircraft approached *Yorktown*. Some were shot down, but six of her Vals hit *Yorktown* with three bombs and Kates scored two torpedo hits. The ship was crippled, and that afternoon her captain gave the order to abandon ship. Meanwhile Spruance, sixty miles away, was taking revenge. Twenty-four Dauntlesses, ten of them transferred from *Yorktown*, dive-bombed *Hiryu*. Four hits sent *Hiryu* the way of her sisters, though it was not until 2.30 a.m. the next morning that she had to be abandoned and sunk by a torpedo from a destroyer.

Yamamoto was slow to realize the catastrophe that had befallen Japan. He was steaming up from the west that evening, hoping for a majestic fleet action. But Spruance was not to be drawn, and had retired to the east. Eventually, in the early hours of 5 June, Yamamoto awoke to the realities of his position and ordered a general retreat. *Yorktown* stayed afloat for two days until the Japanese submarine I.168 found her and put two torpedoes into her. Her sinking at 6 a.m. on 7 June was the last act in the Battle of Midway, in which the United States Navy had won a strategic victory to rank with Salamis, Lepanto and Trafalgar.

6
`Channel Dash'

Scharnhorst, Gneisenau and Prinz Eugen

Events in the Far East might have depreciated the capital ship's status, but in home waters they were still powerful pieces on the sea board. In February 1942 the Kriegsmarine and the Luftwaffe, in a rare bout of cooperation, brought off a neat tactical *coup* which in one dramatic operation showed the strengths and weaknesses of airpower pitted against important heavy ships.

Scharnhorst and *Gneisenau* arrived at Brest on 22 March 1941, after a joint sortie into the Atlantic in which they had sunk 115,600 tons of Allied shipping. On 1 June they were joined by *Prinz Eugen*, after the *Bismarck* episode. There, the three ships were blockaded by sea and air, and were made primary targets for Bomber Command.

By the end of 1941 Hitler had decided that the three ships must return to Germany. They were needed to defeat the plan Hitler fancied the Allies were preparing to invade Norway. He also decided that the best way was the shortest, through the English Channel. The Führer gave his admirals a flat ultimatum: either the ships returned to Germany or they would be paid off in Brest and reduced to hulks.

The Germans prepared very carefully for the breakout. The route was swept of mines and specially marked out with buoys and light-ships. The heavy ships would be escorted by five large and five light destroyers, the screen being augmented by E-boats en route. The Luftwaffe had some 280 fighters, Me.109s, Focke-Wulf Fw.190s and Me.110s, to maintain a constant

The German squadron at sea in the English Channel, February 1942

Lots of struts in all directions,
Curved and cut-out centre sections –
Stringbag the Sailor's had his day,
But in his own distinguished way
He's left his mark on history's page,
The champion of the biplane age!

umbrella of never less than sixteen and sometimes up to thirty-two fighters over the ships. This strength would be increased for the passage through the Straits of Dover. All this would be betrayed by unusual activity on radar screens, but the Germans made skilful use of jamming and electronic counter-measures against radar stations on the south coast.

By January 1942 evidence from various sources suggested that the German ships were getting ready to go to sea. The Admiralty forecast of the German intentions was astonishingly accurate as to their strength, their probable route and their weight of air cover. Only the forecast time of day was wrong. Nobody believed that the German admiral, Ciliax, would dare to lead his force through the Straits of Dover in daylight. In February surveillance patrols were increased, and contingency plans to deal with the breakout were brought forward.

But from the first things went wrong for the Allies. The patrolling submarine *Sealion* most unfortunately missed the German ships when they had formed up and left Brest roads at 10.45 p.m. on 11 February. By radar faults and bad luck, Coastal Command Hudsons also failed to detect the enemy ships. Spitfires actually sighted them the next morning, 12 February, but it was well after 11 a.m. before Admiral Ramsay, the Flag Officer Dover, and the Admiralty had definite news that the enemy ships were at sea. This long delay in reporting the enemy meant that every attempt to stop them was hurriedly mounted, and uncoordinated with other attempts. Small forces had to be thrown into the attack as they became available, to try to inflict at least some damage on the enemy ships before they passed out of range.

Six Swordfish of 825 Sq., commanded by Lt.-Com. Eugene Esmonde, had been moved from Lee-on-Solent to Manston in Kent. It was decided that the Swordfish should attack at 12.45 p.m., which hardly left time for briefing the fighter pilots of Esmonde's escort or for bringing extra fighter squadrons to Manston. Esmonde was supposed to have been escorted by five fighter squadrons, but when the first Spitfires joined him at 12.28 p.m. he decided to go ahead at once and not wait for the others (with a loaded Swordfish top speed of under 90 knots, he knew that unless he hurried he would never catch his targets). Two more fighter squadrons missed Esmonde over Manston, so flew into the Channel and engaged the German fighters as Esmonde made his attack. Two more squadrons looked for the enemy off Calais but failed to find them.

Shortly before Esmonde sighted his targets, five MTBs from Dover tried to attack, but fierce gun and cannon fire from German fighters forced them to fire their torpedoes at ranges of about two miles, and none hit. The MTBs were on the spot, however, to pick up Esmonde's survivors.

Esmonde reached the enemy about ten miles north of Calais. His Swordfish were flying in two flights of three aircraft. His own aircraft was last seen flying over the German destroyer screen in a hail of fire. He was shot down before making his attack and all his crew were lost. The Swordfishes' slow speed baffled the German fighter pilots, who kept on overshooting. They then made their attacks from ahead or astern. The Swordfish air gunners, with rare bravery, stood up in their cockpits and turned round, so that they could advise their pilots of the enemy fighter's movements. Sub.-Lt. C. Kingsmill, R.N.V.R., in Esmonde's flight, flew through intense enemy flak. 'There were more and more large splotches in the sea as aircraft and ships fired at us and their shells burst into the waves. We were really in it now. Suddenly, I felt a sharp pain in my shoulder and my foot went squelchy. Oddly enough I didn't feel any more pain, and managed to keep control of the plane.'[14] Kingsmill's and the other remaining Swordfish, piloted by Sub.-Lt. B. Rose R.N.V.R., dropped their torpedoes before both were shot down. They got no hits. Five men were picked up by the MTBs. The second flight of three Swordfish, led by Lt. J. C. Thompson R.N., were last seen heading for the enemy. All three were shot down. There were no survivors. Esmonde himself was awarded a posthumous Victoria Cross. His body was recovered from the Medway on 29 April.

Meanwhile the German ships were still making steady easting towards home when, at 2.31 p.m. off the Schelde estuary, *Scharnhorst* hit a mine and stopped dead. Ciliax and his Chief of Staff transferred to a destroyer but soon she suffered a premature explosion of one of her own shells and the Admiral moved to a second destroyer. Whilst crossing in the motor-boat, he sat and watched *Scharnhorst*, able to steam again, pass him at 25 knots. To add injury to insult, he and his party were then bombed by a Dornier 217.

The best weapon against Ciliax's ships would have been a massed wave of twin-engined Bristol Beauforts, in their torpedo-bomber role, to do as the Japanese Bettys and Nells had done to Force Z. But Coastal Command had no equivalent of the 22nd Air Flotilla. Their three squadrons of Beauforts were spread about the country, in Scotland, in Cornwall, and at Thorney Island in Essex. All three flew to the scene of action during the day, and all three did their best in attacks through the afternoon and evening. But their attacks were made in small numbers and because of poor visibility, incomplete briefings (through misguided security), radio misunderstandings and the sheer lack of enough aircraft with experi-

Heavily camouflaged German ships
escorting *Scharnhorst, Gneisenau*
and *Prinz Eugen* during the 'Channel
Dash', 12 February 1942

enced enough aircrews, none of their attacks achieved any
success and several Beauforts were lost. Nor did the bombers
do any better. Low cloud prevented attacks from being made
at enough height to use armour-piercing bombs, and the
general purpose bombs which were dropped all missed. High-
level bombing of armoured, fast-moving, manoeuvrable ships
was a specialist task which needed long and careful training.
Bomber Command simply did not have such an arm.

However, the R.A.F. had the last success. That evening
the Germans had good reason to be satisfied with their day's
work. By a combination of excellent advance planning, high
speed, worsening weather, efficient fighter cover, disjointed
enemy opposition and a little bit of luck, the German squadron
had survived attacks by MTBs, by destroyers (from Harwich
that afternoon), and by assorted types of aircraft with guns,
torpedoes and bombs. But at 7.55 p.m., off Terschelling,
Gneisenau struck a mine. She was soon able to steam at 25
knots, but two hours later *Scharnhorst* hit a second mine and
was very seriously damaged. The mines had been laid by
aircraft during the last fortnight, or possibly even that day,
in advance of the enemy's probable track. *Scharnhorst*
struggled into Wilhelmshaven in the early hours of 13 February. *Gneisenau* and *Prinz Eugen* reached the mouth of the
River Elbe later the same day.

Gneisenau was hit by Bomber Command while in the floating dock at Kiel on the night of 26/27 February. Her refit was
abandoned in January 1943 and she ended the war a sad,

German air and sea escort in the English Channel, 13 February 1942

disarmed hulk. *Scharnhorst* went down under the guns of the Home Fleet off the North Cape on Boxing Day 1943. *Prinz Eugen* survived the war, only to be used as a 'guinea pig' in the atomic bomb tests at Bikini in 1946.

It had been a glorious day for Esmonde, and a very busy day for Fighter Command, who had done very well to escort our own aircraft and to attack enemy aircraft and shipping in a very confused tactical situation. But there was precious little credit for anybody else. The news that heavy enemy ships had passed so close to the English coast sent an electric thrill of alarm and outrage through the nation. The Prime Minister set up an enquiry under Mr Justice Bucknill. One of its main conclusions was that the R.A.F. needed proper training for action against shipping. But this, of course, was a matter of R.A.F. policy.

In the end, as the Germans themselves recognized, the successful 'Channel Dash' of Ciliax's ships may have been a tactical victory, but it was a strategic defeat. Those ships were far less dangerous to Allied shipping in Germany than they had been in Brest. Their removal from Brest showed that their position had become untenable there, and that Hitler's thinking had turned to the defensive. Hitler was right on one point. He had always preferred the torpedo to the bomb as a weapon against shipping. In 1938 his naval and air staffs had convinced him of the opposite, probably the only time, he said with sarcastic bitterness, 'they were ever in full agreement'.

7
The
Little Carriers

'Cheap and cheerful'

The loss of *Ark Royal* had been like the end of an era. But a new era had already begun. Aircraft were seen to be prime weapons against submarines, to attack directly with explosives or to guide surface escorts to the spot, or if nothing else to neutralize the submarine by forcing it down until the convoy had passed. It was almost useless and sometimes disastrous for carriers to plunge about the oceans searching for submarines. The U-boats were best fought near their prey, in and around the convoys. Air cover had to be provided above the convoy either by long-range shore-based aircraft or by aircraft from a carrier within the convoy. Convoys did not demand the full pomp and panoply of a fleet carrier. What was needed was some kind of small carrier, something cheap and cheerful.

But at first there were not even enough of these and the Admiralty had to make shift. In the spring of 1941 the old seaplane carrier *Pegasus* and three ex-merchant ships were converted for service as fighter catapult ships. They were used not so much against U-boats as against their partners, the very long range four-engined Focke-Wulf Kondor 200 bombers. After the fall of France the Germans were able to use airfields on the west coast which gave the Kondors a range of 700 miles out into the Atlantic. There they could direct U-boats on to convoys which no longer had surface escorts so far out.

In time, some fifty merchant ships, each carrying one

A Seafire landing on *Formidable*. Note Seafires parked on outriggers

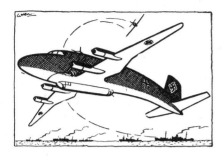

No wonder the Kurier registers pain,
For here's the ubiquitous Hurricane,
Eager to riddle that whale-like hulk,
Which round our convoys desires to
   skulk –
Mammalian monster, soon you'll be
Placed in the "extinct" category!

Hurricane, though still flying the Red Ensign, were commissioned as Catapult Armed Merchant Ships, or CAM ships as they were known. Flying from a CAM ship demanded of the Hurricane pilot a peculiarly cold-blooded kind of courage. On sighting a shadowing Kondor he was launched from his parent ship, fought his engagement above the convoy and then, with very seldom a shore airfield to divert to, he had to bale out or ditch and trust to be picked up from the sea.

The first success by a fighter catapult ship was scored by *Maplin*, whose Hurricane shot down an FW 200C on 3 August 1941. The pilot was Lt. R. W. H. Everett R.N.V.R. (who incidentally piloted Gregalach to win the Grand National in 1929). He got within one and a half miles of his quarry before it noticed him. 'I fired five-second bursts all the way until I was 40 yards astern of the enemy. Another short burst at this range and my guns were empty. I noticed pieces flying off the starboard side of the Focke-Wulf and it appeared to be alight inside the fuselage. I broke away to port at 30 yards. My windshield and hood were covered with oil and I quickly jumped to the conclusion that my engine oil system was badly hit.' The oil was actually from the Kondor, which dived into the sea. 'My one idea,' said Everett, 'was to get down while I still had charge of the situation. I made two rather half-hearted attempts to bale out, but the machine nosed down and caught me when half out. I changed my mind and decided to land in the sea near H.M.S. *Wanderer* and did so. The ship sent a boat and I was extremely well looked after.'[15]

The next development was the Merchant Armed Carrier or MAC ship. These were tankers or grain carriers with a rudimentary flight deck built over their superstructure. The grain ships had a lift and a small hangar and could carry up to four Swordfish; the tankers had slightly longer flight decks but no hangar, and normally carried three Swordfish. Both had a safety barrier and a couple of arrester wires. The ships still flew the Red Ensign, and still carried more than three-quarters of their normal quantity of cargo. The Swordfish were from 836, 840 and 860 Squadrons of the Royal Netherlands Navy, based at Maydown in Northern Ireland. The MAC ship flight decks were minute, being not much wider than the wing span of the Swordfish and so short that an aircraft fully loaded with depth-charges or rockets needed rocket assisted take-off gear (RATOG). There were nineteen MAC ships in service eventually, some convoys in 1944 having as many as four in company. MAC ships' aircraft flew about 4,000 sorties in all, and made twelve attacks on U-boats. No U-boats were sunk, but no convoy with a MAC ship ever lost a ship to U-boats.

The MAC ships were introduced into service in the summer

Supermarine Seafire, introduced into fleet service in 1942. Highly manoeuvrable and a superb fighter ashore, but never really satisfactory flying from carriers: it was always liable to deck crashes, with too weak an undercarrige and too short a range for fleet work. Engine: one 1,470 h.p. Rolls-Royce Merlin 45 Vee type. Span: 36 ft. 10 in. Length: 29 ft. 11 in. Maximum speed: 352 m.p.h. at 12,250 ft. Operational ceiling: 33,800 ft. Normal range: 465 miles. Armament: eight 0.303 in. Brownings, four in each wing, and and later (in 1942) one 20 mm. Hispano cannon and two 0.303 in. Brownings in each wing. The Seafire could carry one 500 lb. bomb beneath the fuselage, or one 250 lb. bomb beneath each wing

of 1943, and were themselves makeshifts. By that time, the true solution to convoy air defence had been evolved, in the auxiliary, or escort carrier. These were small ships, converted from merchantship hulls but still genuine aircraft carriers – although the first auxiliary carrier was herself yet another improvisation. She was the ex-German prize *Hannover*, renamed *Audacity*. She had no hangar, a flight deck 460 feet long, a safety barrier and two arrester wires. She carried six Grumman Martlets and revolutionized the theory and practice of convoy air cover, proving her worth beyond all question in defence of a homeward bound convoy HG 76 which sailed from Gibraltar in December 1941. The convoy surface escort was the 36th Escort Group, with destroyer reinforcements, commanded by Commander (later Captain) F. J. Walker R.N., already a formidable opponent for the U-boats.

Once beyond the range of Gibraltar's aircraft, the convoy had to rely on self-help until they could reach the shelter of home-based Coastal Command, but the combination of *Audacity*'s aircraft and Walker's well-drilled escort team proved devastating. The convoy was soon detected by Focke-Wulf Kondors and as many as nine U-boats closed in for the attack. The main battle lasted four days and four nights. Two

The answer to the Focke-Wulf Kondor: a Sea Hurricane catapulted from the bows of a catapult armed merchant (CAM) ship. Flying these Hurricanes demanded a particular cold-blooded kind of courage of the pilots: once they had fought their dog-fights over the convoy, they had to ditch or bail out. Engine: one 1,460 h.p. Rolls-Royce Merlin XX Vee type. Span: 40 ft. Length: 32 ft. 2¼ in. Maximum speed: 329 m.p.h. at 18,000 ft. Operational ceiling: 35,600 ft. Normal range: 460 miles. Armament: eight 0.303 in. Brownings, four in each wing, or two 20 mm. Oerlikon or Hispano cannon in each wing

Below: H.M.S. *Audacity,* the first auxiliary aircraft carrier, converted from the German prize *Hannover*

Kondors were shot down and four U-boats were sunk around the convoy, one of them, U-131, with the assistance of *Audacity's* Martlets. In exchange, the attacking Martlet was shot down; two merchant ships and the destroyer *Stanley* were sunk.

One more of *Audacity's* Martlets was shot down, by the dorsal gunner of a Focke-Wulf, but the last and saddest loss was the ship herself. On the night of 21 December, during a fierce antisubmarine battle, *Audacity*, against Commander Walker's advice, steamed to the starboard, and most vulnerable side of the convoy, where she was torpedoed and sank. Walker afterwards reproached himself; though *Audacity's* captain, Commander D. W. MacKendrick R.N., was senior to him, he felt that as escort commander he should have ordered *Audacity* to go to port or to remain within the convoy screen. Most of her people were picked up, but MacKendrick was lost.

Escort carriers were desperately needed to fill what was known as 'The Gap', an area of sea about 700 miles across lying like a black pit south-east of Greenland. Here U-boats could operate in comparative safety, out of range of aircraft from the United Kingdom or from North America. The gap was eventually filled, by increasing the range of the surface escorts and perfecting techniques for them to refuel from tankers at sea, and also by allocating very long range Liberators to Coastal Command. But in many ways the escort carriers were the best solution.

The 'Woolworth Carriers', as they were called, were mostly built in America. In January 1941 the Americans began the conversion of their first escort carrier, *Long Island*, and she was ready by June. In May the conversion of the S.S. *Mormacland* to H.M.S. *Archer* was begun, and she was finished by November. Five more C-3 merchant hulls were allocated for conversion. One, U.S.S. *Charger*, was kept in the States for training, the other four became H.M.S. *Avenger, Biter, Dasher* and *Tracker*. The Americans tended to allocate more men for handling and repairing aircraft than the British, but the Admiralty had stricter standards of ship stability and fire precaution. On 15 November 1942, while escorting the 'Torch' landings in North Africa, *Avenger* sustained one torpedo hit and sank after an internal petrol explosion. On 27 March 1943, in the Clyde, *Dasher* blew up and sank with the loss of 378 lives. These two occurrences justified the Admiralty's caution. Before they were passed for service, escort carriers spent many months in British dockyards while major alterations were carried out.

In December 1941 a massive escort carrier building programme was begun. The Americans began the conversion of four fleet oilers to carriers of the *Santee* Class, and twenty C-3

85

Life in the Arctic: flight-deck party clearing snow on _Fencer_, 1944

merchant hulls were allocated for conversion, ten becoming the U.S.N. _Bogue_ Class, and ten becoming the R.N. _Attacker_ class; these ships were 14,000 tons, had a speed of 17 knots, and carried sixteen fighters and twelve torpedo-bombers. In April 1942 twenty more C-3 hulls were allocated, becoming the R.N. _Ruler_ Class. In all, thirty-eight C-3 merchant hulls were turned over to the Royal Navy.

The first charge on the new carriers was air cover for the 'Torch' landings in North Africa, which were given top priority. The landings simply had to succeed. The carriers later provided fighter cover for the assault phases of the landings in Sicily in June 1943 and at Salerno in September. The 'Woolworth Carriers' did not enter convoy service in any numbers until the summer of 1943, by which time the great climactic convoy battles of the North Atlantic had been fought. So the little carriers actually suffered from a shortage of targets. Two U-boats were sunk outright, U-752 by _Archer_ on 23 May 1943, and U-666 by _Fencer_ on 10 February 1944, but escort carrier aircraft also shared in a number of U-boat kills with surface ships.

In the autumn of 1943 *Tracker* and *Fencer* had combined squadrons of Swordfish and Seafires. Their attacks on U-boats were joint efforts. In one, a surfaced U-boat had been found by a patrolling Swordfish and apparently 'took some time to recover from its astonishment at meeting a single-engined biplane in mid-Atlantic'. The U-boat was damaged and two more Swordfish and a Seafire found it still on the surface 'going round in aimless circles. Squadron Commander said on the R/T "Softly, softly catchee monkey" and they cruised round for a minute or two just out of range. Then the Seafire went down and let him have it with m.g.'s and cannon. The Swordfish saw strikes on the conning tower and the guns' crews tumbling off the deck. Then they attacked with depth-charges. The explosions seemed to heave the submarine's bow right out of the water. After that it disappeared altogether for a few moments, then suddenly came up stern first. The stern stuck up out of the white boiling sea like a sharp black rock. A beautiful sight. It sank very slowly, leaving a few survivors swimming about. These were later picked up by one of the sloops. They said the Seafire's first burst had killed their captain. Every time a coconut.'[16]

American CVEs in the Atlantic

The most effective use of escort carriers, or CVEs as the Americans designated them, was in groups, where the carrier herself was accompanied by a permanent screen of three or four destroyers, all forming a separate force under its own captain. The first CVE group was U.S.S. *Bogue*'s, formed in April 1943, followed a few weeks later by groups for *Archer* and *Biter*. The CVE group attached itself to a convoy, flying

Focke-Wulf Fw. 200C Kondor, the long-range reconnaissance bomber of the Luftwaffe which betrayed so many convoys to the waiting U-boat packs. Engines: four 1,200 h.p. Bramo 323R-2 Fafnir radials. Span: 107 ft. 9½ in. Length: 76 ft. 11½ in. Maximum speed: 207 m.p.h. at 15,750 ft. Operational ceiling: 19,030 ft. Normal range: 2,206 miles. Armament: one 20 mm. MG 151/20 cannon in front ventral gondola, one 15 mm. MG 151 machine-gun in forward dorsal turret, three 7·9 mm. MG 15 guns, abeam, and in rear of ventral gondola; 4,630 lbs. of bombs carried internally or externally

Opposite above: 'Cheap and cheerful': the escort carriers *Biter* and *Avenger* coming home after Operation Torch

Below: The merchant aircraft carrier *Ancylus* with two Swordfish (and some collision damage) forward

close cover over the ships, or scouting far ahead and to each side of the convoy. The combination of CVE groups, surface escorts and Coastal Command long-range patrols was a deadly one for the U-boats. The U-boat was often first sighted and attacked by Coastal Command, who would then guide CVE aircraft to the scene, the job being finished by surface escorts. Doenitz insisted on lengthy reports from his U-boats. These talkative targets were easily detected by radio direction finders. Escorts or the CVE group would then run down the bearing until the U-boat was found.

After their defeat in the North Atlantic in April and May 1943, Doenitz withdrew his U-boats from the area and ordered them to concentrate upon convoys in the Central Atlantic. The U-boats were hoping for easier targets and another 'Happy Time' but the American CVE groups were ready for them. They were given a free hand to range about the sea wherever targets presented themselves, hunting down U-boats where direction finders indicated, or even transferring to another convoy if it seemed that it needed extra support. Through tactical experience the CVE groups evolved from a practice of keeping close to a convoy, to a roving commission, and finally to an independent hunter-killer group. It was found unnecessary to keep an air umbrella over the convoy itself. The CVE groups were free to strike at any reported U-boat concentration, so long as they could return to the convoy before the U-boats could reach it. Convoy defence was the vital consideration.

Normally, the first attack was made by a Wildcat fighter, to force the submarine down, whereupon the Avenger TBRs followed up with depth charges, bombs, or latterly, the deadly little homing torpedo Fido. The methods worked wonderfully well. In the last half of 1943, in the calmer waters, lighter winds and generally better weather of the 'horse latitudes', the American CVEs *Bogue*, *Core*, *Santee*, *Card* and *Rock Island* sank twenty U-boats. The top scorer was *Card*'s group, with seven. In mid-July, *Core* and *Santee*, taking it in turns, sank one U-boat a day for four days.

Sometimes the U-boats hurried on their own fates, with mistaken tactics. In June, after one misleadingly successful fight by U-758, Doenitz ordered the U-boats to stay on the surface and fight it out. This, if anything, merely increased their loss rate and in August Doenitz was signalling to his U-boat captains, 'Do not report too much bad news, so as not to depress the other boats; every radio message goes the rounds of the crew in every boat.'[17] But by November, Doenitz had suffered another defeat and had withdrawn all but four U-boats from the Atlantic. Once again he had been forced to try and find easier hunting grounds.

8 Reprieve in the Mediterranean: 1942

Siege and relief of Malta

The withdrawal of *Formidable* in May 1941 and the loss of *Ark Royal* in November deprived the Mediterranean Fleet of an aircraft carrier for many months. Admiral Cunningham was faced by an almost insoluble tactical problem: how to keep Malta supplied without sufficient air power at sea. Malta's fortunes and the progress of the land campaign in North Africa were closely interlinked. If Malta had enough offensive sea and air power to disrupt Axis supply convoys, then the Allies prospered. Conversely, if the Afrika Korps pushed the army back on land, then Malta suffered.

The last months of 1941 were a grim time for the fleet. Besides *Ark Royal*, the battleship *Barham* was torpedoed and sunk by U-331 on 25 November. On 19 December the cruisers and destroyers of Force K, a force which had had some brilliant successes against the Axis, ran into a minefield; the cruiser *Neptune* sank with the loss of everybody on board except one leading seaman, *Aurora* and *Penelope* were damaged, and the destroyer *Kandahar* had her stern blown off and had to be sunk. As if this disaster were not enough, Italian 'human torpedoes' penetrated Alexandria harbour and placed mines under the battleships *Valiant* and *Queen Elizabeth*, putting both ships out of action.

Nevertheless the New Year of 1942 began moderately well. In December Rommel had been forced back to the borders of Tripolitania and the Libyan airfields were once again in Allied hands. In January five supply ships reached Malta, Beau-

S.S. *Melbourne Star,* one of the survivors of the Pedestal convoy, discharging her cargo in Malta, August 1942

Operation Pedestal underway: the Malta convoy of August 1942

Below: Eagle listing heavily to port and sinking after four torpedo hits from U-73, midday, 11 August 1942

fighters of Nos. 252 and 272 Naval Co-operation Groups R.A.F. giving them splendid air cover. But with the Mediterranean Fleet so much reduced by losses the Italian Navy were able to escort supply convoys, and Rommel, too, received reinforcements. On 21 January he launched an offensive which won back the Libyan airfields and forced the 8th Army back to Gazala. Malta came under furious assault again, from North Africa and from Sicily. In February an attempt to run another three ships into Malta failed; none of them got through. A few days later the Axis successfully passed a convoy across to North Africa, with battleships and cruiser cover, in spite of efforts by aircraft from Malta and from No. 201 Group in North Africa to prevent it.

In March Force H sortied from the west and on three occasions *Argus* and *Eagle* ferried a total of forty-seven Spitfires to Malta. On the 20th another convoy of *Breconshire*, *Clan Campbell*, *Talabot* and *Pampas* left Alexandria for Malta, escorted by Admiral Vian, with four cruisers and seven destroyers. Two days later, the convoy was threatened by a strong Italian fleet which included the battleship *Littorio*. In a very gallant action in the Gulf of Sirte, Vian's ships outmanoeuvred and drove off this greatly superior enemy force. But the action had delayed the convoy and prevented it reaching Malta by daybreak. *Clan Campbell* was bombed and sunk twenty miles out. *Breconshire* was disabled and later sank. *Talabot* and *Pampas* actually arrived in Malta only to be bombed and sunk alongside, on 26 March.

On 20 April forty-seven Spitfires were flown into Malta from the U.S.S. *Wasp* but their arrival was seen on radar screens in Sicily and within three days the Luftwaffe had destroyed them all. On 9 May *Wasp* and *Eagle* flew in sixty more Spitfires. In spite of these successes, stocks of food, fuel and ammunition in the island steadily sank and by June 1942 the situation of the people and garrison of Malta was desperate. Two more convoys were sailed, one code-named 'Harpoon' with six merchant ships from the west, the other 'Vigorous' with eleven merchant ships from the east. Both convoys met fierce Axis resistance. 'Vigorous' was threatened, in Vian's words, with 'all known forms of surface attack',[18] including the battleships *Vittorio Veneto* and *Littorio*, and was forced to return to Alexandria. Of the two convoys only two ships from 'Harpoon' reached Malta, with 15,000 tons of desperately needed supplies.

In July the War Cabinet decided that these attempts to relieve Malta were draining away Allied resources without materially helping Malta. It was decided that a relief convoy for Malta must now be given priority over every other naval commitment anywhere in the world. On 10 August, a convoy

The first Fleet Air Arm aircraft ever to land on a U.S. carrier: a Fairey Swordfish, piloted by Lt.-Com. G. A. L. Woods, landing on *Wasp*, 21 April 1942

of fourteen merchant ships, including the tanker *Ohio*, steamed westwards through the Straits of Gibraltar. They were escorted by a powerful force, under Vice-Admiral Syfret, of the battleships *Nelson* and *Rodney*, the carriers *Victorious*, *Indomitable* and *Eagle*, with *Furious* carrying more Spitfires for Malta, seven cruisers and thirty-two destroyers. This convoy, Operation Pedestal, was to be one of the most spectacular convoy actions of the war.

The Axis knew of the convoy the moment it appeared in the Mediterranean and a line of U-boats was spread out in its path. U-73 had the first success, at midday on 11 August, hitting *Eagle* with every torpedo of a salvo of four. She sank in about seven minutes, with the loss of 200 of her people.

At 8 p.m. that evening the first serious air attack developed, of some thirty-five Ju.88s from Cagliari in Sardinia. They were driven off in a short action at dusk. One of *Indomitable*'s Hurricane pilots, Lt. Hugh Popham R.N.V.R., was 'scrambled' and flew across the convoy while it was putting up an intense flak barrage: 'The sight took our breath away. The light was slowly dying, and the ships were no more than a pattern on the grey steel plate of the sea; but where we had left them sailing peaceably through the sunset, now they were enclosed in a

The tanker *Ohio*, deck
almost awash, being
triumphantly towed into Grand
Harbour, Malta, August 1942

sparkling net of tracer and bursting shells, a mesh of fire.
Every gun in fleet and convoy was firing and the darkling air
was laced with threads and beads of fire.'[19]

The nearer the convoy approached to Sardinia the more
often aircraft were launched against them. An attack of
nineteen Ju.88s was beaten off early on the morning of the 12th,
but a much more sustained and serious attack began at noon
and lasted for nearly two hours. Over a hundred aircraft of
various types took part, including Ju.88s, Me.110s, SM.79
bombers, Caproni fighter-bombers, a radio-controlled 'suicide'
Savoia 79 armed with a heavy bomb which fortunately
exploded somewhere in North Africa, and two Reggiane 2000
fighter-bombers which looked very like Hurricanes and joined
Victorious's landing circuit; they dropped bombs, one of which
landed on *Victorious*'s flight deck but, again most fortunately,
it failed to explode. None of these attacks nor a simultaneous
attack by SM.79s with torpedoes achieved anything, but a
force of over thirty Stukas hit the merchantman *Deucalion*
with one bomb and she had to be sunk.

That evening the Italian U-boat *Cobalto* was depth-
charged and forced to the surface where she was rammed and
sunk by the destroyer *Ithuriel*. But the convoy was now

Though in front three engines cluster,
All the power they can muster
Isn't really half enough
To pull along such ill-shaped stuff
As the Sparviero flies—
Christmas tree of Southern skies.

within range of the more deadly Luftwaffe squadrons based in Sicily, who bombed and damaged *Indomitable* so badly her aircraft had to be transferred to *Victorious*. They also sank the destroyer *Foresight*.

At dusk the convoy was attacked by the Italian U-boats *Dessie* and *Axum*. One outstandingly successful salvo of three torpedoes from *Axum* hit (probably) the cruiser *Nigeria* which had to return to Gibraltar, the anti-aircraft ship *Cairo* which had to be sunk, and *Ohio* which caught fire but steamed on. The capital ships and the fleet carriers had turned back as previously arranged when the convoy neared the Sicilian Narrows, leaving the convoy under the command of Rear-Admiral Burroughs in *Nigeria*. The admiral now had to shift his flag to the destroyer *Ashanti*. As he was doing so the convoy came under another attack by about eighty bombers, sinking the merchantmen *Empire Home* and *Clan Ferguson* and damaging the *Brisbane Star*, which was able to keep going. The Italian submarine *Alagi* then put a torpedo into the cruiser *Kenya*. The convoy was in a state of utter confusion, in a storm of gun-flashes, explosions and tracers, with ships steering in all directions to avoid bombs, torpedoes and each other.

By midnight the convoy had restored itself to some order and was rounding Cape Bon, when it was attacked by German and Italian E-boats, lying in wait close inshore. Their torpedo attacks were the most devastating yet. Four merchant ships were sunk and the cruiser *Manchester* was disabled. She was scuttled next day (prematurely, as a later court martial decided).

At dawn on 13 August, the convoy was on its last lap. The bombing attacks from bases in Sicily intensified as the convoy neared its destination. A bomb detonated the petrol and ammunition on board the freighter *Waimarama* and the ship completely disappeared in a great sheet of flame, leaving a handful of survivors swimming in the sea. *Ohio* was damaged again by a Ju.88 which crashed on to her forecastle. Unbelievably, she was hit a third time, by a Stuka which lodged on her poop. Her engines broke down and she came to a dead stop in the water. Another merchantman, the *Dorset*, was sunk before the convoy reached Malta that evening. *Port Chalmers*, *Rochester Castle* and *Melbourne Star* were the only three surviving merchantmen. They were joined the next day by the still struggling *Brisbane Star*. But the great prize was *Ohio*, with her 10,000 tons of petrol and kerosene. She was taken under tow and brought into Grand Harbour amid tremendous rejoicing, on the 15th. The Pedestal convoy had lost an aircraft carrier, two cruisers, a destroyer and nine merchant ships. A second aircraft carrier, two cruisers

Above: An Italian torpedo plane dropping its torpedo

Right: A Swordfish based at Alexandria dropping a depth-charge, 1941

The U.S.S. *Ranger* (CV-4) underway
in 1942

and three merchantmen had been damaged. Against that, the convoy had sunk two Italian submarines and shot down about forty aircraft.

Malta had been reprieved, though not relieved. By the end of November the island was again in desperate straits and its surrender to the enemy was actually under discussion. That month another convoy, code-named 'Stoneage', sailed from Port Said unnoticed and unremembered (although the cruiser *Arethusa* was very badly damaged during its passage and had to be towed through a gale to Alexandria). With a second convoy, 'Portcullis', in December, Malta was finally saved.

Operation 'Torch'

Even before Malta was made secure, the centre of strategic interest in the Mediterranean had already shifted westwards to the landings in North Africa in November 1942. The war was at a turning point. The German Sixth Army was held at Stalingrad. The Afrika Korps was in retreat from El Alamein. Operation Torch was the first strategic offensive by the Allies in the west. Times had changed since *Ark Royal* operated alone off Dakar in 1940. For 'Torch', Force H had *Formidable*, *Victorious* and *Furious* to cover the landings. *Furious* was detached on 8 November to join the escort carriers *Biter* and *Dasher* in the Centre Naval Group at Oran; *Argus* and *Avenger* operated with the Eastern Naval Task Force at Algiers. In all, the F.A.A. fielded 130 fighters for 'Torch' to give air cover and close support for the landings until airfields ashore were secured and R.A.F. and U.S.A.A.F. aircraft could

H.M.S. *Victorious:* with her sister ships *Formidable* and *Illustrious*, *Victorious* had a speed of 31 knots, carried 36 aircraft, a complement of 1,400 men, and was the first class of ship to have an armoured flight deck

be flown in from Gibraltar. Thirty Albacores were also embarked, in case the Italian Fleet attempted to molest the landing forces. For their landings on the Moroccan coast the U.S.N. had the large carrier *Ranger* and four escort carriers and provided fighter cover and strikes at Port Lyautey, Casablanca and Safi. There was very little opposition to any of the landings from Vichy fighters, and it was soon overcome. At sea, *Avenger* was sunk whilst escorting a withdrawing convoy. Albacores from *Victorious* and *Formidable* shared two U-boat kills.

The 'Torch' landings showed that small carriers, if there were enough of them, were an excellent means of giving close fighter support in places where the Allies did not have shore airfields near enough. After 'Torch' the carriers went on to cover the assault phases of the landings at Salerno in September 1943 and in the south of France in August 1944. At Salerno things went awry for the Allies and for a time there was a real chance that the landing force might be driven back into the sea. The heavy guns of the fleet held the ring, and the fleet Seafires gave fighter cover when there were no other fighters available. For three days the Seafire squadrons in *Attacker, Battler, Hunter, Stalker* and the repair carrier *Unicorn* drove themselves until they literally had no aircraft left. When the war moved to the Far East, the little carriers, now actually known as assault carriers, gave fighter support for the East Indies Fleet's operations off the Burmese Arakan Coast, for the capture of Rangoon, the landings at Penang and the taking of Singapore, although these last two operations took place after the Japanese surrender.

9 The U-Boat Menace

The Battle of the Atlantic

The Battle of the Atlantic began on 3 September 1939 and lasted until the German surrender in May 1945. Perhaps battle is too small a word for what happened. It was a war, as Churchill said, a war of groping and drowning, of ambuscade and stratagem, of science and seamanship, and while it lasted it engaged thousands of men on both sides, serving in hundreds of ships, submarines and aircraft operating over ten million square miles of ocean. Those who took part in that struggle could think of nothing else. Those who were not part of it could not imagine what it was like. It was the one strategic battle on which all others depended and maybe, like the siege and capture of Troy, it is too big for the scope of the historian and requires instead to be celebrated by a great artist.

The battle could not have been won without the shore-based aircraft of Coastal and Bomber Commands, and the U.S. Navy and Army Air Forces. The vital battles around the Atlantic convoys in the spring of 1943 swung the Allies' way after air cover was extended across the whole Atlantic. At one crucial point, the struggle against the U-boats was nearly lost for want of a few dozen more very long range aircraft. But most fortunately the right decisions were made, and in time. When the final figures were analysed, shore-based aircraft sank more U-boats than any other arm while at the same time weakening the enemy's war effort with a steady toll of surface shipping sunk and damaged by bombs, torpedoes and airlaid mines.

A U-boat sinking after gun and depth-charge attack by Sunderlands. Survivors can be seen in the water bottom right; the U-boat sank a few seconds later

Atlantic convoy

Coastal Command

Coastal Command was formed in 1936 and given its somewhat misleading title, which covered only some of its duties. The Command entered the war with as many handicaps (some self-imposed) as most branches of the Allied war effort. There were very few aircrews with any training in either attacking or defending shipping. There was no properly equipped long-range ocean search aircraft, nor any aircraft suitable for either task of defence or offence against shipping. There was no torpedo strike force, except one squadron of antique Vickers Vildebeeste biplanes. The standard coastal reconnaissance aircraft was the twin-engined Avro Anson. It was, in its way, a splendid aircraft and, as they said, 'Anson is as 'Andsome does', but it was already obsolescent in 1939. It was soon supported and then replaced by Whitley and by Wellington bombers, and by American-built Hudsons. In the Short Sunderland the Command had a first-class long-range flying boat. When fully equipped later in the war the Sunderland was a bruising opponent for the U-boats. Its very successful American counterpart, which saw service with many Coastal Command squadrons, was the Catalina.

At the outset Coastal Command had no effective airborne submarine-killing weapon. Prewar the R.A.F. had placed an unjustified faith in their antisubmarine bomb. There was no proper bomb-sight for it, and the weapon itself was ineffectual under action conditions. Nevertheless the Air Ministry looked askance at the depth-charge and, incredibly, in April 1940, decided not to develop it further. Luckily this decision was reversed and depth-charges were again fitted that summer. A much modified and improved depth-charge entered service in the spring of 1941.

Mines laid from the air proved to be a very potent weapon against shipping, but full advantage could not be taken for a long time because the most profitable waters for mine-laying were furthest away, in the Baltic and Scandinavian waters. The only aircraft which could reach these waters were in Bomber Command, who preferred to bomb Germany instead. Postwar analysis showed that the R.A.F. could have contributed much more by air mine-laying than by bombing, but not only did the R.A.F. continue to bomb Germany but actually, for a time in the first months of 1941, discontinued mine-laying.

There were restrictions on where and when Coastal Command could attack until as late as March 1941. Not until then was Coastal Command given permission to attack enemy or enemy-controlled shipping at any time and anywhere. Furthermore, there were still those (and by no means

Above: Short Sunderland, long-range flying boat, which joined the R.A.F. in 1938 and did not retire from service until 1958. Fully armed it was a prickly proposition, known to the Germans as the *Stachelschwein,* the porcupine, and with bombs and depth-charges it was a bruising opponent for the U-boats. Engines: four 1,010 h.p. Bristol Pegasus XXII radials. Span: 112 ft. 8 in. Length: 85 ft. 8 in. Maximum speed: 210 m.p.h. at 6,500 ft. Operational ceiling: 17,900 ft. Range with maximum load: 1,780 miles.
Armament: four 0.303 in. Brownings in tail turret, one 0.303 in. Vickers K or Lewis in nose turret, two Vickers Ks amidships, and up to 2,000 lbs. of bombs or depth-charges

all of them worked at the Air Ministry) who could not grasp that the Navy's task was to protect shipping, not shipping lanes. The controversy between convoy and the 'safe patrolled route' was finally resolved, in favour of convoy, late in 1940.

The R.A.F.'s somewhat ambivalent attitude towards Coastal Command made them very reluctant to transfer aircraft to Coastal. It was conceded that aircraft had an important part to play in the war at sea, but nothing ever really shook the R.A.F.'s determination that it was far better to bomb Germany than to attack U-boats in 'the vast distances of the sea', as some senior R.A.F. officers liked to call them. Both Bomber and Coastal Commands had some notable successes against enemy heavy shipping, which severely embarrassed the German naval staff, but the conviction still lingered that these were only diversions from the proper task of bombing Germany. Obviously, it was hard for the R.A.F. to understand that a stick of bombs which, for example, delayed *Scharnhorst* and *Gneisenau* sailing had a greater proportionate effect for its weight on the enemy's total war effort than if it had hit any other target (unless, conceivably, it had hit and killed Hitler himself).

Throughout the war, experience showed that the closer the liaison between ships and aircraft the better. For instance, when East Coast convoys came under attack by the Luftwaffe, cries for help often brought Fighter Command to the scene in the wrong place, or after the attackers had left. The real solution, which the Air Ministry eventually conceded, was a radio-equipped surface escort ship to 'direct' the incoming fighters on to the enemy. This innovation, with a system of 'grades' of fighter cover protection, gave the most important cargoes the closest cover.

So, slowly and painfully, the realities of air power at sea made themselves felt. In April 1941 Coastal Command was placed under the operational control of the Admiralty, though remaining part of the R.A.F. This in time brought about a degree of co-operation and mutual understanding between the two services which was never even remotely approached by their German and Japanese counterparts.

Coastal Command's operational policies were several times defined and redefined, with new emphasis and re-emphasis, in a series of directives issued from time to time. But the final definition must be the long and magnificently impressive list of tasks that Coastal Command undertook over the years in the face of ignorance, prejudice, failure to reach correct decisions in the face of the clearest evidence, and difficulties of divided command. In 1940 Coastal Command had had to give priority to North Sea patrolling, looking for the expected German invasion fleet. As the threat of invasion receded, Coastal Command could give more attention to the Atlantic, while still on the lookout for German heavy ships making for the convoys. In April 1941 fuelling bases were established in Iceland and the first squadrons of Hudsons were soon based there. By May convoys could be given air escort to distances of 700 miles from the United Kingdom, 600 miles from Canada, and 400 miles south of Iceland. But that black 'gap' still yawned for some time to come.

The first joint air-surface sinking of a submarine was by the escorts *Fowey* and *Whitshed* and a Sunderland of No. 229 Squadron, who together sank U-55 in the Western Approaches on 30 January 1940. Bomber Command destroyed U-31 in the Heligoland Bight on 11 March. In time, Bomber and Coastal Command aircraft, with American aircraft of the Army and Navy, carried a vast arsenal of different weapons against the U-boats: depth-charges, rockets, batteries of cannons and machine-guns, and mines to lay across the

Consolidated B-24 Liberator: in 1943 a few score of these very long range aircraft enabled convoys to have air cover all the way across the Atlantic, and thus helped to turn the battle in the Allies' favour. Engines: four 1,200 h.p. Pratt and Whitney R-1830-43 Twin Wasp radials. Span: 110 ft. Length: 66 ft. 4 in. Maximum speed: 303 m.p.h. at 25,000 ft. Operational ceiling 28,000 ft. Maximum range: 4,600 miles. Armament: two 0.50 in. Brownings in dorsal turret, and seven 0.303 in. Brownings in the nose (four in tail turret, one on each beam) and up to 8,000 lbs. of bombs or depth-charges

U-boat pen entrances. Some aircraft had very bright Leigh lights, to find surfaced U-boats at night. Some had magnetic anomaly detectors, to pick up the magnetic field disturbances of a U-boat's submerged metal hull. But the main weapon was persistence, that sense of unrelenting, unremitting pressure of surveillance, which gave a U-boat captain the hair-prickling feeling that his boat was never safe, surfaced or dived, and he could never relax, by day or night.

The aircrews' main enemy was boredom. They flew for many hours, in all weathers, over empty seas. Many of them never saw a U-boat, and seldom an enemy of any kind. They flew until they had hallucinations, taking violent action to avoid mountain ranges in mid-ocean, sighting rows of mysterious lights, or finding themselves flying alongside motor-cyclists, fairground steam-engines, or the Flying Scotsman. They had to stare for hour after hour at unbroken blackness, seascapes which never changed, radar screens which never showed an echo. As numbness and cold took possession of their bodies, they relied on dead reckoning and the compass to bring them back to base, firesides, warmth and human movement.

R.A.F. Mosquitos sinking a U-boat in the Atlantic

Attack on *Scharnhorst* and *Gneisenau*

A few of those long, bleak days had bright, glorious flashes. In March and April 1941 Coastal Command joined in the blockade of Brest by air and sea to prevent *Scharnhorst* and *Gneisenau* returning to join *Bismarck* in Germany. At first light on 6 April, a Bristol Beaufort of 22 Squadron Coastal Command, piloted by Flying Officer Kenneth Campbell R.A.F.V.R., made a lone torpedo attack on *Gneisenau*, who was secured alongside in the inner harbour, protected by a stone mole and by massed rows of anti-aircraft guns. The ship was difficult to approach from the air. Even if an aircraft succeeded in making an attack the pilot would find it almost impossible to pull up because of rising ground behind the ship. It must be assumed that Campbell was aware of this, but he pressed home a low-level attack and hit *Gneisenau* with his torpedo, causing severe damage aft below the waterline. Campbell and his crew were lost. Campbell himself was awarded a posthumous Victoria Cross. Photo-reconnaissance showed *Gneisenau* had been moved into dry dock. Both ships were bombed and hit by Bomber Command a few nights later. Neither was able to join *Bismarck*.

Coastal Command's Beauforts had another success in the early hours of 13 June 1941, when they attacked the German battleship *Lutzow* off southern Norway. A Beaufort piloted by Flt.-Sgt. Lovitt hit *Lutzow* with one torpedo and brought her to a standstill. Other torpedo and bombing attacks by Blenheims failed, but the Germans were taken aback by what they themselves called the 'superb dash' of the attacks. *Lutzow* got under way again. But her planned breakout into the Atlantic was cancelled.

Little Beau-Fort likes dangerous sport
And knows just where to find it—
Trust it to roam and it'll come home
And leave a wreck behind it.

U - boat capture

At about 6.30 a.m. on 27 August 1941 a Hudson of 269 Squadron captained by Sq.-Ldr. J. H. Thompson, patrolling from Iceland, sighted the swirl and wake of a U-boat. The Hudson marked the position with smoke floats and, when the submarine surfaced shortly afterwards, attacked with depth-charges. But the charges hung up and the U-boat dived once more. A second Hudson had arrived on the scene by the time the U-boat surfaced again. This time the depth-charges did explode and the U-boat 'was completely enveloped by the explosions and shortly afterwards submerged completely'. Two minutes later it shot to the surface and 'ten or twelve of its crew wearing yellow life jackets appeared on the

Battle of the Atlantic: a 1,200 ton U-boat under attack by U.S. naval aircraft

Following pages: U-570 captured by Hudson aircraft in mid-Atlantic and brought back under her own power by a British crew, September 1941

conning tower and came down on deck'. The Hudson swept the U-boat's upper deck with machine gun fire. Seven minutes later 'a white flag was seen to be waved'. (This was actually the captain's shirt, which was 'lightly starched and had frills down the front').[20] Throughout the rest of the day and the following night, Hudsons and Catalinas kept watch over the surrendered submarine, until a destroyer arrived to take her in tow. The U-boat U-570 was captured with priceless intelligence and cryptographic information still on board. She later saw service as H.M.S. *Graph*.

Bay of Biscay offensive

The progress of the war had established that in general it was better to attack U-boats near the convoys. Coastal Command departed from that principle by carrying out an offensive against U-boats on their transit routes to the north of Scotland and in the Bay of Biscay. The Bay was a special killing ground where the battle swayed to and fro as one side gained a tactical or technological advantage. Wellingtons fitted with Leigh lights and an early form of radar attacked and damaged three U-boats in June 1942, and sank two in July. The Germans suspected the existence of a new device and fitted U-boats with a rudimentary detector. The Bay 'offensive' more or less came to a stop in October. It began again in January 1943 but paused when the U-boats were fitted with 'Metox' radar detector. In March Coastal Command had aircraft fitted with the new ten centimetre radar and the offensive began in earnest. One U-boat, U-376, was sunk in April, but this sinking taken with

other reports from damaged U-boats convinced Doenitz that the Allies had some mysterious kind of detection gear and he ordered U-boats to submerge all night, surface in daylight to recharge batteries and if attacked to fight back. This was a bad blunder. In May seven U-boats were sunk in the Bay. Two more collided and sank each other.

The Allied aircraft had the support of Captain Walker and his escort group in the Bay. By contrast, U-boats had very meagre air cover, due to the long-standing feud between Goering and Doenitz. But the Allies, too, had their disagreements. The Admiralty asked for the transfer of long range Lancasters from Bomber to Coastal Command to assist in the U-boat war, but were turned down. In July 1943 U.S. Liberators and Catalinas joined the R.A.F.'s Wellingtons, Halifaxes and Sunderlands in the Bay and using radar, magnetic anomaly detectors, depth-charges, rockets and Leigh lights in one hectic month sank 16 U-boats, nine of them in six days. In August the Luftwaffe began to give fighter cover and to use glide bombs against the surface escorts, while the U-boats found a safer route to the south, where the shadow of the Spanish Pyrenees mountains gave them some protection against radar. Again, the Bay battle came to a halt. Doenitz then made another error in believing that 'Metox' was betraying his boats, and ordered it to be taken out. In November the offensive began once more, so that between May and December 1943, 32 U-boats transiting through the Bay were sunk.

However, in that same period, 258 U-boats entered and 247 left the Bay to and from French ports, so the percentage sunk by the Bay offensive was not unduly high. Meanwhile, from May to December, 183 U-boats were sunk in areas other than the Bay. So the Bay offensive did not necessarily prove that it was best to leave the convoys, and go out and search for the U-boats. But it did have a powerful psychological effect on the Germans, who could never discover until much later how or why they were losing so many U-boats.

Victory in the Atlantic

In February 1943 the figures of losses to U-boats soared: they sank 63 ships, of 359,328 tons. In March the U-boats did even better: 108 ships, of 627,377 tons. But that same month enough very long range Liberators were allocated to Coastal Command to close at last the infamous mid-Atlantic 'gap'. It was no coincidence that in April and May the situation in the Atlantic dramatically changed. A series of great convoy battles was fought which decisively defeated the U-boats and turned the tide in favour of the Allies. Those battles fought

in the wastes of ocean, in 25° West and 50° North, had no names, no famous headstones to hang legends on, but they were in their way as critical as Midway and Stalingrad. From March to May the Axis lost, from all causes, 71 German and 6 Italian U-boats; 36 of them were sunk by aircraft. The loss rate was too high, and the U-boat offensive in the North Atlantic was temporarily abandoned.

In the tremendous manpower expansion needed in wartime, Coastal Command drew its aircrews from several nationalities and from all walks of life. Kenneth Campbell was a chemistry graduate from Clare College, Cambridge. His navigator was a Canadian from Toronto. His wireless operator was a Somerset farmer and his air-gunner a chauffeur from Edmonton in North London. On 11 August 1943, Flying Officer Lloyd Trigg D.F.C., R.N.Z.A.F., an agricultural machinery salesman from Houhora, New Zealand, was flying a Liberator of 200 Squadron West Africa Command from Rufisque, Dakar, on patrol when he sighted U-468 on the surface. The U-boat did not dive but took the Liberator under very accurate anti-aircraft fire as Trigg approached to attack. The Liberator was soon set on fire and its tail was enveloped in flame but Trigg pressed his attack at fifty feet above the sea and sank the U-boat with a perfectly placed straddle of bombs. The Liberator flew on and crashed in the sea, killing Trigg and all his crew. The U-boat captain and some of his ship's company were later picked up (floating in one of the Liberator's rubber dinghies) and it was on their recommendation and warm admiration of Trigg's conduct that he was awarded a posthumous Victoria Cross, the first of the war for sinking a U-boat.

In the end, Coastal Command's achievements have to be rendered down into lame statistics. They began in September 1939 with sixteen squadrons of about 250 aircraft, and most of those Ansons. They ended the war in May 1945 with nearly seventy squadrons, most of them British, but some American, some Canadian, Australian, Norwegian, Czech, New Zealand, South African and Polish. They had well over a thousand aircraft of all types, 500 for use against the U-boats, 300 for use against enemy surface shipping and another 250 for photo-reconnaissance, meteorology and air-sea rescue. Shore-based aircraft sank 254 submarines and shared another thirty-six in all theatres during the war. Of those Coastal Command sank 189, shared twenty-four and damaged another 385. They also sank about half a million tons of enemy shipping, and rescued nearly 6,000 Allied aircrew, 277 enemy aircrew and nearly 5,000 civilians from the sea. It cost Coastal Command 2,000 of their aircraft and nearly 9,000 of their own air and ground crews.

10
Operations in the Arctic

The life and death of *Tirpitz*

When, in A. P. Herbert's words, Hitler 'leaped upon his largest friend' and attacked Russia in June 1941, it soon became necessary for the Allies to send supplies to Russia by sea round the North Cape. Whatever the political and moral justification for the Russian convoys, as naval undertakings they were always basically unsound. The merchant ships and their escorts had to make their way to and from north Russian ports along a route often restricted by polar ice, and always within easy reach of enemy air, U-boat and surface ship bases, where heavy Allied covering forces could not protect them. To the dangers of the enemy was added the appalling ferocity of the Arctic weather.

The first convoy sailed in August 1941, escorted by the old carrier *Argus*. Meanwhile the fleet carriers of the Home Fleet operated in northern waters, *Furious* and *Victorious* striking at Petsamo and Kirkenes in July 1941, and *Victorious* again at targets in the Bodö area in September. But these were not much more than pinpricks. It was not until March 1942 that aircraft from *Victorious* carried out a strike which was to have a profound and far-reaching effect on German tactics in the Arctic. On 8 March *Victorious* was with the Home Fleet providing deep cover for the convoy PQ12. *Tirpitz* had been reported at sea and was steaming southward, having missed the convoy. At 6.40 a.m. the C.-in-C., Admiral Tovey, ordered *Victorious* to fly off six searching Albacores, who were followed at 7.30 a.m. by a strike of twelve Albacores armed

The German battleship *Tirpitz* under attack from Albacores from *Victorious* (note torpedo tracks in the background) off Norway, 8 March 1942; all the torpedoes missed

Tirpitz lying heavily camouflaged in a Norwegian fjord, February 1942

with torpedoes, led by Lt.-Com. W. J. Lucas R.N. At 8.02 *Tirpitz* was sighted by an Albacore, and she at once altered course to the east and increased speed for safety at Vestfjord about fifty miles away. Lucas himself sighted *Tirpitz* at 8.42, to the south-east of him, range about twenty miles. With a maximum speed of 155 knots, flying into a near headwind of about 35 knots, the Albacores took time to overhaul their fast-moving target. The first attack was at 9.20 and although all the Albacores dropped their torpedoes and succeeded in attacking *Tirpitz* from both port and starboard sides, they scored no hits, to the great disappointment of themselves, *Victorious* and the rest of the Home Fleet. Lucas had not previously flown with his squadron, who had had very little practice in carrying out a difficult combined attack. Photographs suggested that the torpedoes had been dropped at too great ranges. However, although *Tirpitz* was unhurt, Hitler himself decided that she would never go to sea again when there was any chance of an aircraft carrier being against her. So Lucas's strike had an important effect on the mind of the enemy.

But this restriction was unknown to the British Admiralty and when *Tirpitz* again put to sea in July 1942, to attack the convoy PQ17, the mere rumour of her presence had the most melancholy results. *Tirpitz*'s sortie was soon over and she

Fairey Barracuda, two-seater dive/torpedo-bomber, an ungainly and somewhat unsatisfactory aircraft which, however, had one glorious battle honour – the attacks on *Tirpitz* in the summer of 1944. The Barracuda shown here has missed the arrester wires and is crashing into the safety barrier. Engine: one 1,600 h.p. Rolls-Royce Merlin 32 Vee type. Span: 49 ft. 2 in. Length: 39 ft. 9 in. Maximum speed 228 m.p.h. at 1,750 ft. Operational ceiling: 16,600 ft. Range with torpedo: 686 miles. Armament: two 0.303 in. Vickers K guns in rear of cabin; one 1,650 lb. torpedo, or one 1,000 lb. bomb, or four 450 lb. depth-charges, or six 250 lb. bombs

never came near PQ17, but the convoy was ordered from London to scatter. The order had a disastrous effect. Deprived of mutual support and covering gunfire, the hapless merchant ships were individually snapped up by U-boats and the Luftwaffe. Of twenty-two ships lost in the convoy, twelve were sunk by bombers and torpedo-bombers, who had a major success in conditions admittedly made easy for them.

The next convoy, PQ18, was delayed until September, because of the need to provide ships for 'Pedestal' and to wait for longer nights. The escort carrier *Avenger*, with twelve Sea Hurricanes and three Swordfish, joined on 9 September off Iceland. After a poor start on the 12th, when massed torpedo-bombers of Luftflotte V from Norway penetrated the screen and sank eight merchant ships while the fighters were out of position, the Hurricanes fought a week-long battle with the Luftwaffe so well that not another ship was lost until *Avenger* herself had entered Kola Inlet, when two more were torpedoed. The Hurricanes were 1Bs, an early type, although ironically the convoy had later and faster marques of Hurricane in crates in their holds. Admiral Tovey protested at this illogicality, which did not happen again. Nevertheless the Hurricanes shot down five German aircraft and damaged twenty more. Four Sea Hurricanes were lost, three of them to over-enthusiastic fire from the convoy. The Hurricane of the

Right: H.M.S. *Victorious* at sea

Below right: The Fleet Air Arm attack on *Tirpitz:* the smoke-screens to hide the battleship are drifting across the waters of the fjord

Following pages: The Fairey Firefly, a two-seater fighter, took part in the strikes against *Tirpitz* and later saw service with the British Pacific Fleet. The Firefly shown overleaf has just made an emergency landing on H.M.S. *Indefatigable.* Engine: one 1,730 h.p. Rolls-Royce Griffon IIB Vee type. Span: 44 ft. 6 in. Length: 37 ft. $7\frac{1}{4}$ in. Maximum speed: 316 m.p.h. at 14,000 ft. Operational ceiling: 28,000 ft. Maximum range with auxiliary tanks: 1,070 miles. Armament: two 20 mm. Hispano cannon in each wing; one 1,000 lb. bomb or four 60 lb. rocket projectiles

CAM ship *Empire Morn* shot down two Heinkel He.115 torpedo-bombers on 18 September.

Aircraft sank thirty-two ships in Russian convoys in 1942, but no more until 1945, when one ship was lost. However, escort carriers did not sail regularly with Russian convoys until early in 1944, because of the overriding needs of first 'Torch' and then the Atlantic convoys. *Dasher* joined Convoy JW53 in February 1943 but had to retire after two days because of bad weather damage. *Chaser* did the round trip to Russia and back with JW/RA 57 in February and March 1944, when her aircraft sank two U-boats and shared a third with *Onslaught.*

It was on the number of U-boats sunk that the escort carriers had their most dramatic effect. The four British built escort carriers *Activity, Nairana, Vindex* and *Campania* were especially successful in the Arctic. From March 1944 to May 1945 these four, with *Tracker, Fencer,* and *Striker,* between them sank seven U-boats and shared in three more. The Swordfish was by far the most successful U-boat killing aircraft, because it was the only one that could be operated safely

from the narrow decks of the CVEs by night; the American Avenger was bigger, stronger and more comfortable for the aircrews, but was very seldom operated at night. The weather made flying conditions very difficult for all the aircrews. They flew for many hours in darkness or in the opaque grey of an Arctic winter day, through blizzards and fierce Arctic gales. In that intense bitter cold, depth-charge safety release clips froze solid at critical attacking moments and there were many gun stoppages and rocket misfires. After their sorties, when they were often short of petrol, the pilots had an anxious search for their carriers, which were hidden in fog banks or sudden swirling snow storms. In that weather the ship would be pitching and tossing furiously, burying her bows in the sea and throwing up sheets of spray which froze as it drifted down. The crew of any aircraft which went over the side had to be rescued in a very few minutes, before they froze to death. Aircrews were often so numb with cold that they had to be lifted bodily out of their cockpit seats by the flight deck handlers. Some eighty aircraft were lost while escorting the Russian convoys, most of them in flight deck landing mishaps.

On 6 September 1943 *Tirpitz* with *Scharnhorst* in company bombarded shore installations on the island of Spitzbergen. It was the first, last, and only time that *Tirpitz*'s main armament fired at a surface target in anger: she never sailed again on another operation, but retreated to her northern fastness. But thenceforth she had more effect upon the war than she ever had by going to sea. Her presence lay like a giant shadow across the route to Russia and the larger North Atlantic. Lying in her fortified lair in a Norwegian fjord, *Tirpitz* became, like Grendel's mother, a creature of legendary menace and supernatural powers. Hidden both by Arctic mists and by clouds of rumour, she swelled ever more monstrous and dangerous the more the Allied naval staffs thought about her.

Such a dragon could not be left unmolested, and throughout her career *Tirpitz* was always a prime target for all branches of Allied arms, not just the Royal Navy and the R.A.F., but also the Russian Air Force and the Norwegian resistance. Hampdens of Bomber Command had attacked *Tirpitz* while she was fitting out in Wilhelmshaven in the autumn of 1940. Bomber Command attacked her again at Trondheim three times in the spring of 1942, without doing her any damage, and losing twelve bombers. In September 1943 midget submarines penetrated *Tirpitz*'s anchorage in Kaafjord and severely damaged her with mines laid under her keel.

By the following spring intelligence reports suggested that *Tirpitz* had been repaired and was almost operational again. That summer the Fleet Air Arm carried out what can only be

A big ship needed a big weapon;
Lancaster bombers of R.A.F.
Bomber Command finally sank
Tirpitz with 12,000 lb. Tallboy
bombs in November 1944. Engines:
four 1,280 h.p. Rolls-Royce Merlin
33 or 22 Vee types. Span: 102 ft.
Length: 69 ft. 4 in. Maximum
speed: 287 m.p.h. at 11,500 ft.
Operational ceiling: 24,500 ft.
Range with 12,000 lb. bomb:
1,730 miles. Armament: eight
0.303 in. Brownings, two in nose
and dorsal turrets, four in tail
turret

The wreck of the *Tirpitz*, Tromsö

described as a campaign of air strikes to try and disable her.

The fleet's main bomber for the *Tirpitz* strikes was the Fairey Barracuda, which had first seen active service at Salerno the previous year. It was an ungainly looking aircraft with a somewhat 'Christmas tree'-like appearance when it was fully fitted out with bombs, lifeboats and radar aerials. It had a disconcerting habit of suddenly and unaccountably plunging out of the sky. The Barracudas were escorted by squadrons of new American-built Hellcat and Corsair fleet fighters; these were excellent aircraft, faster, more robust, more heavily armed and armoured than the Seafire, and by that stage they were rolling off American production lines by the thousand. In July a new British fighter-bomber for the fleet, the Fairey Firefly, made its operational debut.

The first strike, code-named 'Tungsten', was the largest operation so far undertaken by the Fleet Air Arm. The aircrews had trained intensively, with special exercises, and had studied models of the fjords and countryside around *Tirpitz*. The Navy had come a long way since Esmonde and his six Swordfish. Some 160 aircraft took part in 'Tungsten', launched

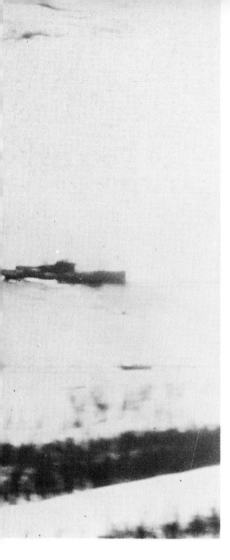

from two fleet carriers, *Victorious* and *Furious*, and four CVEs, *Emperor, Searcher, Pursuer* and *Fencer*. There were two waves of twenty-one and nineteen Barracudas, escorted by twenty Wildcats, twenty Hellcats and ten Corsairs.

The first aircraft attacked at 5.30 a.m. on 3 April 1944, just as *Tirpitz* was making ready to go to sea for exercises. Whilst the fighters strafed flak positions and *Tirpitz*'s upper-deck and superstructure, the Barracudas of the first wave scored ten direct hits; the second scored five. Eight hits were with 1,600 lb bombs, and five with 500 lb bombs. There were two near misses. *Tirpitz* suffered quite severe splinter damage to her superstructure, and over 400 casualties amongst her ship's company.

In May Barracudas from *Victorious* and *Furious* were thwarted by low cloud and could not carry out an attack. In July *Formidable, Indefatigable* and *Furious* tried again with a massive strike of forty-four Barracudas, eighteen Corsairs, twelve Fireflies and eighteen Hellcats. *Tirpitz* had fifteen minutes' warning and the Barracudas had to attack through smoke-screens and furious flak. They scored no hits. In four operations in August 1944 (code-named 'Goodwood I-IV') *Indefatigable, Formidable, Furious, Nabob*, and *Trumpeter* launched strikes in which a total of 220 aircraft were involved. Many enemy aircraft were shot down but the Barracudas only scored two hits, on 24 August. One 1,600 lb armour-piercing bomb penetrated to *Tirpitz*'s keel, but failed to explode. *Nabob* was torpedoed by a U-boat, but despite heavy flooding aft reached harbour successfully.

Hard though they tried, the Fleet Air Arm could not deliver a really crippling blow against *Tirpitz*. A big ship needed a big weapon and on 15 September the R.A.F. delivered it. Twenty-seven Lancasters of No. 9 and 617 (Dambuster) Squadrons flying from Yagodnik in Russia, dropped sixteen 12,000 lb Tallboy bombs and seventy-two mines. In spite of the target rapidly disappearing in smoke, they got one hit with a Tallboy from 12,000 feet, right forward on *Tirpitz*'s bows. That was enough. The Germans decided not to repair the ship and moved her to Tromsö. There, she was just within range of bombers from the United Kingdom and on 29 October twelve Lancasters scored a near miss which bent *Tirpitz*'s port propeller shaft. There was now no chance whatsoever of the great ship going to sea again, but naturally the Allies did not know this. Finally, on 12 November, thirty-two Lancasters of No. 9 and 617 Squadrons administered the *coup de grâce*. They dropped twenty-nine Tallboys, with two direct hits and one near miss close on the port side. After extensive flooding and listing, followed by an explosion in the after magazine, *Tirpitz* capsized, with great loss of life.

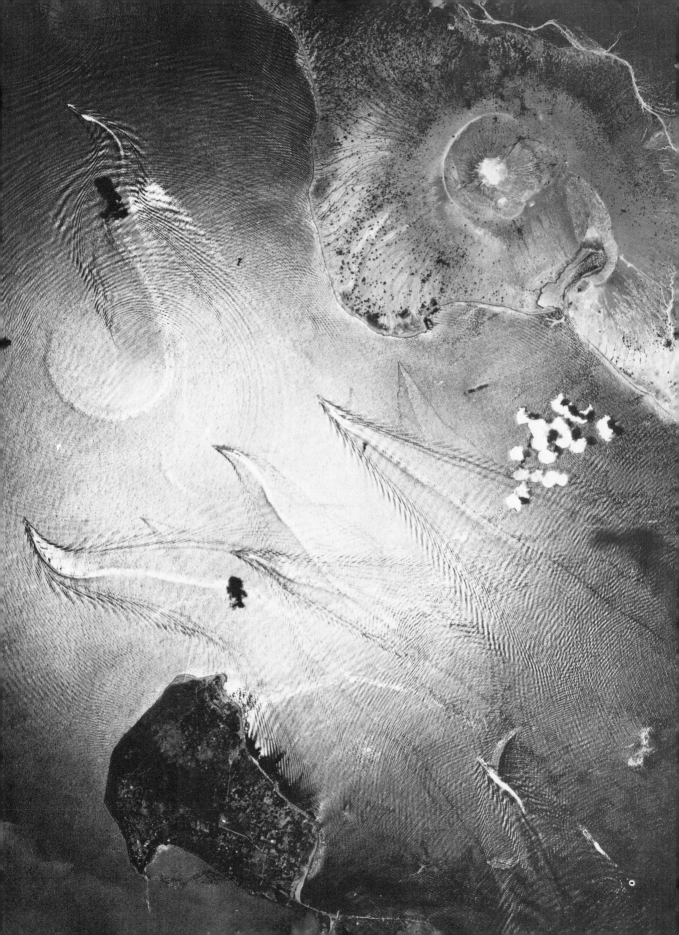

11 Allied Counter-Attack in the Pacific

Guadalcanal to Japan

The victory at Midway, coming as it did like a brilliant flash of light at a dark time for the Allies, prompted thoughts of some form of defensive counter attack in the area of the Coral Sea. But the strategic situation was complicated (as it always was in the Far East) by the fact that there were two separate commands: Admiral Nimitz's Pacific Ocean Command, and General MacArthur's South-West Pacific Command. It was sometimes difficult for outsiders to credit that these two great commands were devoted to fighting the enemy and not each other; to go between them was like passing from one autonomous feudal kingdom to another, crossing a frontier bristling with mutual antipathies and suspicions. The Coral Sea area was in MacArthur territory, while the ships and troops for the campaign were administered by Nimitz, who was very reluctant to commit his ships, especially his few precious remaining carriers, to MacArthur's proposal for a direct assault on Rabaul. A compromise was reached: Nimitz would command an assault on the Santa Cruz Islands and the seaplane base at Tulagi and, when a base had been established, MacArthur would take command and direct a dual assault through Papua and the Solomons, eventually converging on Rabaul. Plans were advancing when Australian coast-watchers in the islands reported that the Japanese had begun to build an airstrip on the island of Guadalcanal, in the Solomons.

Guadalcanal was hot, humid and unhealthy, with thick

Japanese shipping in Rabaul Harbour twisting and turning to avoid bombs from Liberators and Mitchells

jungles, malarial swamps and a rough uncomfortable spine of mountains. But it was strategically invaluable, and both sides knew it. On 7 August 1942 the 1st U.S. Marine Division landed on Guadalcanal and on Tulagi. The Tulagi landing was fanatically resisted by the Japanese (an ominous foretaste of things to come) but the landing on Guadalcanal itself was only lightly opposed. The Marines soon captured the airstrip and named it Henderson Field, after a Marine hero of Midway.

Guadalcanal controlled the Coral Sea and the approaches to Australia and New Guinea, and control of Guadalcanal developed into a race to see which side could build up its forces on the island faster. This largely depended upon which side held local air mastery and this, in turn, virtually meant the possession of Henderson Field.

Japanese naval reaction to the landings was swift and savage. In the early hours of the night of 8/9 August Admiral Gunichi Mikawa, with a force of seven cruisers and one destroyer from Rabaul, made one anticlockwise sweep at high speed around Savo Island, off Guadalcanal. A mixed force of Allied ships defending the troop transport anchorages was caught unawares and dispersed, and, inexperienced in the neglected arts of night-fighting, lost the American cruisers *Astoria*, *Quincy* and *Vincennes*, and the Australian cruiser *Canberra*, all shelled, torpedoed and later sunk after a short but vicious engagement. This was a defeat for the Allies comparable to that inflicted on the Italian Navy off Matapan. It established the Japanese 40 knot oxygen-powered 'Long Lance' torpedo as a formidable weapon, and it dispelled once and for all any notions that the Japanese were a myopic people with poor night vision.

The disaster, though bad enough, might have been worse. Mikawa withdrew without attacking the troop transports, although they had been his primary target and were at that time at his mercy. Mikawa feared an attack by American carrier aircraft at first light, when in fact Vice-Admiral Frank Fletcher, commanding the Expeditionary Force, had taken the carriers away from Guadalcanal the previous day, a decision which is still controversial.

Deprived of carrier air support and with their surface cover badly mauled the night before, the Amphibious Force also left Guadalcanal the next day. The 17,000 Marines on the island were left to fend for themselves for the time being. They had Henderson Field ready by the 20th and fighters were flown in from the carrier *Long Island*. With these few, almost symbolic, aircraft the Allied counteroffensive in the East properly began. It was these wings, multiplied by thousands, which took the Allies to Tokyo Bay.

The Japanese were already fighting one campaign in Papua,

and they seemed slow to admit that another major campaign had begun on Guadalcanal. The first of many destroyer convoys, which under Rear-Admiral Raizo Tanaka became known as the 'Tokyo Express', sailed on the night of 18/19 August with about 2,000 troops, which the Japanese believed would be enough. The first of several bloody repulses, at the Tenaru River on 21 August, awoke them. A larger convoy, of four destroyers and Tanaka's flagship the cruiser *Jintsu*, sailed on the 21st and were covered by the whole Combined Fleet, which Yamamoto had brought down to Truk, and which included some very familiar names. There, again, were *Shokaku* and *Zuikaku*, with Nagumo himself in command. The carrier admiral was Hara, flying his flag in *Ryujo*. The whole force was commanded by Kondo, flying his flag in the cruiser *Atago*, and it had all the familiar Japanese trappings of a Vanguard Force of battleships and cruisers and, inevitably, a diversionary 'decoy' force, in this case, *Ryujo* and her cruiser and destroyer escort.

Such a concentration of Japanese ships was soon detected and the Allied Task Force 61 (which also contained some familiar names) moved into the area east of the Solomons. Fletcher was in overall command, with the carriers *Enterprise*, *Saratoga* and *Wasp*, and the battleship *North Carolina* which had been specially fitted (a sure sign of the new Pacific times) with a greatly increased weight of anti-aircraft fire.

Battle of the Eastern Solomons

The coming battle, known as the Battle of the Eastern Solomons, followed the pattern of previous carrier engagements: both sides searching for the other, followed by strike and counterstrike. On 23 August, when Fletcher was to the north-east of the Solomons, reconnaissance detected Tanaka's troop convoy 300 miles to the north, steaming south. Fletcher at once launched a strike from *Saratoga*, but Tanaka had only waited for Fletcher's reconnaissance plane to fly away before reversing course himself. *Saratoga*'s strike could not find the target and landed on Henderson, rejoining their ship the next day. Fletcher meanwhile believed that there was a lull in the battle and so detached *Wasp* to the south to refuel. In fact, the main Japanese fleet reversed course again during the night, and the next day, the 24th, was to see the climax of the battle. At 10 a.m. a shorebased aircraft reported a carrier group (actually *Ryujo* with her escort) some 300 miles to the north of Fletcher. On this occasion, the decoy worked and Fletcher ordered *Enterprise* to launch an armed reconnaissance at this target. There was now no doubt that Japanese carriers were operating north of the Solomons and once again, as at the Coral Sea, Fletcher sent off his main striking force (from *Saratoga*) without being sure of his enemy's whereabouts. There followed a very confused period, with the air filled with conflicting radio reports as various aircraft sighted parts of the Japanese fleet. *Enterprise*'s aircraft attacked and did minor damage to *Shokaku*. *Saratoga*'s strike found *Ryujo*, the decoy, hit her several times with bombs and one torpedo, so that she sank later that day.

Fletcher had not been wholly deceived. He had sent off his bombers with no escort, keeping his fighters back against the attack he knew would come. His ships prepared for the onslaught to fall upon them. Fuel lines were drained, hatches secured. The ships were battened down as though against a typhoon. Shortly after 4 p.m. radar detected a mass of aircraft approaching from the west. Fletcher flew off all his fighters, and launched his remaining bombers and torpedo-bombers on a counterstrike.

The art of fighter control had been much improved since the early days. Well directed from *Enterprise*, the Wildcats wreaked a tremendous carnage amongst the Japanese attackers. Those that penetrated were greeted with a colossal barrier of gunfire from *North Carolina* and the other ships. Nevertheless handfuls of Vals got through and hit *Enterprise* with three bombs. She came to a stop, while the Japanese bombers

were frantically searching for her only fifty miles to the west. Happily, she was able to get under way again and rejoin TF 61. Meanwhile, two dive-bombers and five Avengers with torpedoes from *Saratoga*, unable to find *Ryujo*, came upon Kondo's force and very badly damaged the light carrier *Chitose* who only just managed to make harbour in Truk.

Tanaka had still been grimly pressing on towards Guadalcanal. Early on the 25th his convoy was sighted and attacked by Marine dive-bombers from Henderson Field who had actually been looking for the Japanese carriers. The Marines were joined by Flying Fortresses from Espiritu Santo. Three of Tanaka's ships were sunk and the convoy had to turn back. This, rather than the loss of *Ryujo*, was the real defeat suffered by the Japanese.

Once again a tactical draw was really a long-term strategic gain for the Allies. More of Japan's irreplaceable experienced aircrew strength had been drained away, while the industrial might of the U.S.A. was still increasing its output. New carriers were growing on the slipways, new aircraft rolling off the lines, hundreds of fresh pilots were being trained in the clear weather, warm climate and calm skies of the southern States of the U.S.A.

Now, as both sides strove furiously to build up their resources on the island, there came to be a curious state of balance over Guadalcanal. By day carrier fighters and the Marines from Henderson held the air. By night the initiative returned to the Japanese and the redoubtable Tanaka continued to run his Tokyo Express down the 'Slot', as the channel between the Solomon Islands was called.

Ironically, Japanese submarines achieved successes denied to their aircrews. On 31 August, about 250 miles south of Guadalcanal, *Saratoga* was torpedoed by I.26 and put out of

The U.S.S. *Saratoga,* with her characteristic funnel, in the Pacific, 1942

Above: A Grumman F6F-6 Hellcat, the best carrier fighter of the war: very fast, very manoeuvrable, easy to land on deck, capable of taking punishment, the Hellcat won a great victory in the Philippine Sea in June 1944. Engine: one 2,000 h.p. Pratt and Whitney R-2800-10 Double Wasp radial. Span: 42 ft. 10 in. Length 33 ft. 7 in. Maximum speed: 375 m.p.h. at 17,300 ft. Operational ceiling: 37,300 ft. Normal range: 1,090 miles. Armament: three 0.50 in. Browning M-2s in each wing

Opposite: Japanese shipping under bombing attack by U.S. aircraft in Rabaul Harbour, 2 November 1943

action for three months. A fortnight later, *Wasp* was hit by three torpedoes from I.16. There was severe flooding, fierce fires broke out, and the ship had to be abandoned, to be sunk later by the Japanese. The Japanese failed to read the strategic lesson: some of the resources and fuel they were to expend upon their kamikaze offensive might have been better invested in submarines.

After the Battle of the Eastern Solomons and the misadventures to *Wasp* and *Saratoga*, the U.S. Navy was left with only one serviceable carrier, *Hornet*. Japan had four. Now, if ever, was the time to avenge Midway. The chance of revenge seemed to come at the end of October 1942, when the main Japanese fleet of four carriers, five battleships, fourteen cruisers and forty-four destroyers was operating off the Solomons in support of the land campaign on Guadalcanal. The Japanese had succeeded in raising their strength on the island almost to parity with the Americans. The Marines on Henderson were subjected to bombardment by night and air attack by day. By 20 October the Japanese must have felt that one more heave would give them the vital airfield. But the Marines resisted dourly and were still holding out when the last of the carrier confrontations of 1942, the Battle of Santa Cruz, took place on 26 October.

Santa Cruz

The Allies now had a much more aggressive commander at sea, in Vice-Admiral Halsey, who took over as C.-in-C. South Pacific on 18 October. It was probably Halsey's spirit for the offensive and his ceaseless yearning to 'Kill more Japs, Kill more Japs', as his slogan said, that convinced the Japanese that the Allies had more strength at sea than they actually had.

Opposite: A Zeke just missing the U.S. carrier *Sangamon,* December 1943

For Santa Cruz Halsey had *Hornet* and *Enterprise*, frenziedly repaired just in time, under the command of Rear-Admiral Thomas Kinkaid, whom Halsey ordered to advance boldly in support of the Marines on Guadalcanal with a wide sweep around the Santa Cruz islands. At midday on 25 October Catalinas sighted two Japanese carriers about 400 miles north of Kinkaid, heading south-east. That afternoon, Kinkaid launched a strike northwards, but the Japanese had reversed course. Flying Fortresses and Catalinas attacked with bombs and torpedoes, without success.

Kinkaid stood on to the north during the night. His opposing fleet commander, Kondo, was heading south, so as to be in position for his carriers (once again under Nagumo) to fly off aircraft as soon as the army announced they had taken Henderson Field. The distance between the two fleets was rapidly shrinking, when two Catalinas attacked *Zuikaku* with torpedoes. They missed, but Kondo decided to turn back for the time being. As so often in 1942, the main action took place soon after first light, when both sides sighted each other at about the same time. Aircraft from *Hornet* and *Enterprise* put the small carrier *Zuiho* out of action. *Shokaku*, so often in the wars, was battered again so badly she was not operational for another nine months. For their part, Nagumo's aircrews hit *Hornet*, with yet another long established train of events: fires, flooding, abandonment, and *coup de grâce* from four Long Lance torpedoes.

Afterwards, the same picture of a Japanese Pyrrhic victory presented itself. The Japanese Navy had to attack, and to keep on attacking, and each victory was a defeat in the end. The Americans had lost another carrier and were once more reduced to one. But Santa Cruz had taken another terrible toll of Japanese aircrews. Yamamoto had barely a hundred serviceable aircraft, only enough to operate *Junyo* and *Hiyo*. The Marines still held Henderson Field.

In the series of ferocious surface night actions, carrier engagements and torpedo attacks in the Guadalcanal campaign which came to a temporary pause in the action off Tassafaronga on 30 November, so many ships were lost that the narrow waters of the 'Slot' around Savo became known as 'Ironbottom Sound', and the stretch of sea between San Cristobal and Espiritu Santo, 'Torpedo Junction'. In these battles the Allies lost *Hornet* and *Wasp*, seven cruisers and eight destroyers. The Japanese lost *Ryujo*, the battleships *Hiei* and *Kirishima*, a cruiser and six destroyers. There was also on both sides a long list of carriers, battleships, cruisers and destroyers damaged, some so badly they were never operational again.

As the months passed, the Americans were able to build up

Admiral William ('Bull') Halsey

their strength at a rate which the Japanese, despite Tanaka, could never match. By December 1942 the Americans had some 40,000 troops on Guadalcanal, the Japanese about 25,000. But while the Americans had increased by another 10,000 by February 1943, the Japanese had dropped to about 12,000. Reluctant as they were to abandon the island, the Japanese at last realized that Guadalcanal had become a costly and open-ended commitment. Raizo Tanaka, running his Tokyo Express in reverse, began to take off troops. By 7 February, under the Allies' very noses, he had spirited away the last Japanese from Guadalcanal. The Allies had gained the vital island. By then, Australian and American troops in Papua had also inflicted upon the Japanese their first reverse on land, by forcing them back along the Kokoda Trail across

the Owen Stanley mountain range to Buna, on the north coast of New Guinea. Clearly, the rising sun had passed its high noon.

This defeat in New Guinea so embarrassed and irritated the Japanese that on 28 February 1943 they embarked a complete infantry division of some 7,000 troops in a convoy of seven transports, a collier and eight destroyers and dispatched them to New Guinea. On 2 March the convoy was sighted crossing the Bismarck Sea. In a two-day battle, high-level bombers of the U.S.A.A.F. and R.A.A.F. sank the entire convoy and four of the destroyers. This Battle of the Bismarck Sea, as it was known, was a tremendous and timely victory for land based bombers.

New offensive in the Solomons

In March 1943 Admiral Yamamoto arrived in Rabaul to direct personally a new offensive in the Solomons, Operation I. In late 1942 and early 1943 Yamamoto had four and some-times five carriers to the Americans' one. Pardonably, he had missed his chance. But now he went on to make a gross strategic error by ordering his naval aircrews ashore and using them to attack the now heavily defended Henderson Field, and other targets along the north coast of Australia and Papua, at Milne Bay and Port Moresby. The aircrews vastly overestimated their successes. In fact, a few small ships were sunk and a few Allied aircraft were destroyed, at the cost of still more of Yamamoto's priceless aircrews. He would have done far better to have held these crews back against the day, which was bound to come, of another clash with Halsey's and Spruance's carriers.

The Yamamoto ambush

In April 1943 Yamamoto went on a tour of inspection of the western Solomons. Through intercepted signals his route was betrayed and on the 18th the Sally carrying him and his staff was ambushed over southern Bougainville by a squadron of Lightning fighters from Guadalcanal. The Sally was shot down, and none of the passengers or crew survived. So passed the great architect of the early Japanese victories. His death was in its way symbolic of Japan's declining naval air power.

In October 1942 the U.S. Chiefs of Staff had become so

alarmed at their shortage of aircraft carriers that they asked for the loan of one – better still two – British carriers to operate in the Pacific. The request was awkwardly received in London and for a time there was a slight breakdown in communications between the Allies. The true American predicament was not immediately appreciated by the Admiralty, who in any case had many other commitments, world wide. The outcome of 'Torch' was still in doubt and it was not until well into December that one carrier, *Victorious*, could be spared. She reached Pearl Harbor in March 1943 but naturally had to retrain her ship's company and aircrew in American practice and American aircraft, and did not join the U.S. fleet until May. She and *Saratoga* operated with Halsey's Third Fleet in the summer and although there were no more great carrier battles, *Victorious* took part in the covering operation for the landings of MacArthur's forces in New Georgia, before returning home via the U.S.A. in September 1943.

Dual strategy in the Pacific

General MacArthur's naval forces in the South-West Pacific were redesignated the Seventh Fleet in March 1943, and were commanded first by Admiral Carpender and later by Kinkaid. Supported from the sea by the Seventh Fleet which had its own force of CVEs, and transported by the Seventh Amphibious Force under Rear-Admiral Daniel Barby, MacArthur's troops advanced upon Rabaul on two fronts, with a sequence of combined operations along the north coast of New Guinea, and in the Solomons. By December 1943 they had invaded Nassau Bay, Lae and Finschafen, and Cape Gloucester in New Britain; in the Solomons they had landed at New Georgia, Vella Lavella and Bougainville. The land actions were accompanied by yet another series of hard-fought sea fights, and by still more attrition of Japanese aircrews. It was estimated that the Japanese lost some 2,500 aircraft attempting to recapture Guadalcanal and in the subsequent defence of the Solomons.

MacArthur's offensive was one half of a two-pronged thrust at Tokyo, the other half being Nimitz's 'island-hopping' in the Central Pacific. Both 'prongs' required tremendous air support from carriers and to the end of his days General MacArthur complained bitterly that his advance was only allocated the 'little' carriers, while the main carrier force operated in the Pacific. In theory, the U.S. Chiefs of Staff favoured Nimitz's offensive. In practice, both went on together. But there is no doubt that, in the end, the Chiefs of Staff allocated the carriers to the right theatre.

General MacArthur had promised the people of the Philippines that he would return. To the General, any attack on metropolitan Japan by any route which left the Philippines still in Japanese hands was unthinkable. The axis of MacArthur's advance, known as the 'Army' plan, was therefore through New Guinea to the Philippines, to Formosa or Okinawa, and thence to Japan. Nimitz's axis, the 'Navy' plan, was across the islands of the Central Pacific.

The Navy plan had many advantages. It was a shorter route to the Japanese heartland. It would provide bases for very long range bombing of Japan at an earlier stage. It would avoid a series of protracted land campaigns under very difficult climatic and geographic conditions (the suicidal resistance of Japanese garrisons was already showing how protracted such campaigns would be). Most important of all, Nimitz's plan would make the fullest use of air and sea power, departments of war in which the Allies were growing stronger in the Pacific with every month.

It was very unfortunate that the two plans became so closely associated with the 'Army' and the 'Navy' because they tended to inflame the traditional rivalries between the two services.

The Fifth Fleet

For most of 1943 there was a comparative lull in the Central Pacific. It was as though the theatre was awaiting the entrance of the queen of Pacific sea battles, the *Essex* Class aircraft carrier. These splendid new 27,000 ton, 32 knot vessels were designed for the offensive, having unarmoured flight decks but carrying ninety, and later a hundred, aircraft on board. The first of them arrived at Pearl Harbor in May 1943 and by the autumn the Central Pacific Fleet, known from January 1944 as the Fifth Fleet, had six heavy carriers, including a new *Yorktown* and a new *Lexington*, five *Independence* Class light carriers, twelve battleships, a host of cruisers, destroyers and landing craft of various types and sizes. The fleet commander was Raymond Spruance, now promoted Vice-Admiral.

The Fifth Fleet was the largest, most powerful, most flexible and self-sufficient weapon in naval history. It used naval air power on a global scale, combining extraordinary mobility with tremendous hitting power, able to strike at one target and then vanish into the distances of the Pacific, using the very vastness of the ocean as a defence, before striking at a second target hundreds of miles away a short time later. The fleet's striking tip was the Fast Carrier Task Force, designated Task Force 58 and commanded by Rear-Admiral

Marc Mitscher. TF 58 was deployed in four separate task groups, each group normally having two heavy and two light carriers, and each having its own escort of fast battleships, cruisers and destroyers. Task groups could operate together as one force, or single groups could be detached to refuel and rearm independently, whilst the rest maintained continuous pressure on the enemy.

During the drive across the thousands of miles of the Central Pacific, TF 58's brief was to seal off a target atoll from all Japanese interference while the landing was in progress, by striking at distant Japanese island bases to prevent them flying on reinforcements, by pre-invasion strikes on the target atoll's defences, by giving tactical air support to the troops approaching the beaches during the assault phase, and by intercepting Japanese attempts by sea or air to molest the troops on the target.

Whilst TF 58 held the distant ring, the Marine and Army assault troops – the Fifth Amphibious Corps, under Major-General Holland Smith – were transported to the target beaches by Rear-Admiral Richmond Turner's Fifth Amphibious Force, which was another large fleet of transports, cargo ships, landing ships and craft, escorted by its own carriers, battleships, cruisers and destroyers. The Fifth Fleet also had its own land based air force, under Rear-Admiral John Hoover. The fleet had no permanent bases. A mobile Service Force of tankers, repair ships, tenders and floating docks set up floating bases in island lagoons to the rear of operations. The targets were tiny coral atolls which had nothing on them of any assistance to the fleet. Every single item of supply had to be brought to the spot. So, to the art of war the Fifth Fleet brought the science of logistics, on a titanic scale.

The 'Atoll War'

The 'Atoll War' began on 20 November 1943 with an assault on the Gilbert Islands, where the U.S. Marines had a bloody initiation on the beaches of Tarawa. They suffered some 3,000 casualties before the island was secured on the 23rd. Next were the Marshalls, two hundred miles to the north-west. After a thunderous preliminary bombardment (a lesson learned from Tarawa) the major atolls of Kwajalein and Roi-Namur were assaulted on 1 February 1944 and secured by the 4th, after a fanatical resistance by the Japanese who fought literally to the last man. The remaining major atoll in the Marshalls was Eniwetok, to the west, but before it was assaulted TF 58 raided Truk, Saipan, Guam and Wake Island. Truk was very heavily attacked on 17 and 18 February.

Eniwetok was attacked on the 23rd and taken in three days, again after unbelievable resistance by the Japanese garrison.

Three months after the Atoll War opened, the Japanese had been forced to abandon their outer defensive line extending to the Bismarcks and withdraw to an inner line a thousand miles to the west, running from the Marianas to the Palaus to western New Guinea. Scores of islands east of this line stayed in Japanese hands until the end of the war. They were simply bypassed and allowed to wither on the vine. Their garrisons, supplied (if at all) only by submarine, were depleted by starvation, disease, and by repeated air attacks from Fifth Fleet carrier air groups new to the Pacific using them as 'live' practice targets.

In the New Year of 1944 MacArthur still pressed forward, taking Saidor in January, the Admiralty Islands in March and sidestepping the main Japanese 18th Army at Wewak, landing further along the coast at Hollandia in April. For these operations, MacArthur did have the help of the Fifth Fleet carriers, who demonstrated how rapidly they could bring force to bear on the required spot. Growing ever more confident of their ability to operate within range of Japanese air bases, TF 58 sped southwards and secured MacArthur's seaward flank in March and April with further crushing attacks on Truk, the Palaus and the western Carolines, forcing the main Japanese fleet to a new base at Singapore.

At their next objective in May, the large offshore island of Biak, MacArthur's forces found the Japanese strength and opposition much greater than expected. The reason was that Biak's airfields were needed by the Japanese in their plans for one more decisive confrontation with the American fleet.

The plan, Operation A-GO, was devised by the new C.-in-C. Admiral Soemu Toyoda, who had replaced Koga, Yamamoto's relief, when he himself was killed in an air crash. In A-GO, a 'special force' would lure the American fleet to some position off either the Palaus or the western Carolines,

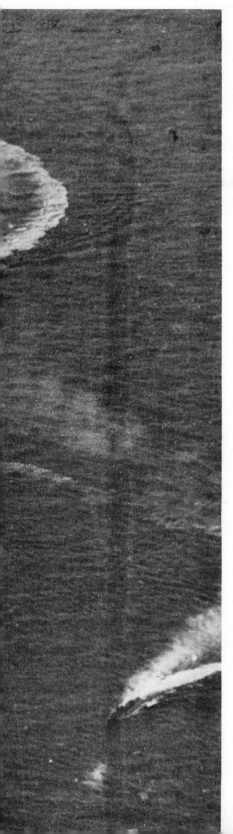

where it would be within range of the maximum number of Japanese air bases. The enemy would then be crushed between the hammer of the Japanese fleet and the anvil of Japanese shorebased air power.

As usual, the Japanese plan was complicated, and relied upon the enemy doing the right thing. But it was of only academic value. At that stage in the war the Japanese were no longer capable of imposing any plan upon the Allies. They could only look for success if Spruance made a mistake.

Battle of the Philippine Sea

On 11 June 1944 TF 58 began to soften up the defences of the Marianas with a mighty fighter sweep of over 200 Hellcats. The next day two groups struck at Saipan and Tinian, while one pounded Guam. That evening two groups broke away, raced 650 miles north to destroy Japanese aircraft on Chichi Jima and Iwo Jima. At the same time heavy battleships opened a bombardment on airfields and installations on Saipan and Tinian. Caught by surprise, the Japanese High Command awoke to the realization that the Allies were about to assault and capture the Marianas. This was a threat to the Japanese heart. Saipan was the naval and administrative centre for the outer defence ring. The Gilberts and Marshalls could be lost, even the great fortresses of Rabaul and Truk could, if necessary, be left to their fates. But the Marianas must be held. If Saipan fell Japan's defeat would follow. As Admiral Turner's troops waded ashore on Saipan on 15 June the Japanese main fleet sailed from their temporary anchorage at Tawi Tawi in the Suli Archipelago. A detachment under Rear-Admiral Ugaki, including the two 60,000-ton battleships *Yamato* and *Musashi* which had gone south to Batjan to support the hardpressed Japanese troops in New Guinea, was also recalled and ordered to rendezvous with the main fleet.

The Allies were now about to reap the rewards of their intelligent use of naval air power. They had won such supremacy over such vast areas of the Pacific that two huge invasion armadas, one carrying 71,000 troops from Hawaii to assault Saipan, and the other of 58,000 troops from Tulagi and Guadalcanal to assault Guam, had been able to assemble, sail, and reach their destinations without being molested.

The Japanese Mobile Fleet, commanded by Vice-Admiral Jisaburo Ozawa, met Ugachi on 16 June, some 300 miles east of the Philippines. The van of the fleet, led by Vice-Admiral Kurita, was formed in three groups around the three

A huge tubby body, a slim Davis wing,
Of Reuben Fleet's baby let us praises sing,
Tho' from the Pacific and a weapon of War,
The Atlantic knows well our good Liberator.

light carriers *Chiyoda*, *Chitose* and *Zuiho* (with eighty-eight aircraft). Although very strongly escorted, by four battleships, five cruisers and eight destroyers, Kurita's force was intended as bait, to draw the American fleet within range of the main body 100 miles in the rear. The main fleet was formed in two groups each with three carriers: Group A, with 207 aircraft, in Ozawa's flagship *Taiho*, *Shokaku* and *Zuikaku*; and Group B, with 135 aircraft, in *Junyo*, *Hiyo* and the light carrier *Ryuho*. Ozawa had a total force of nine carriers, five battleships, nine cruisers, twenty-four destroyers, and 473 aircraft, including seaplanes.

Between Ozawa and Saipan lay Spruance's Task Force 58, a great fleet spread out over 700 square miles of sea, with fifteen carriers, 956 aircraft, seven battleships, twenty-one cruisers and sixty-nine destroyers. The Task Groups were: TG 58.1, *Hornet* and *Yorktown*, with the light carriers *Belleau Wood* and *Bataan*; TG 58.2, *Bunker Hill* and *Wasp*, with the light carriers *Monterey* and *Cabot*; TG 58.3, *Enterprise* and *Lexington*, with the light carriers *Princeton* and *San Jacinto*; and TG 58.4, with *Essex* and the light carriers *Langley* and *Cowpens*. Curiously, even now, and even Spruance, had a vestigial belief in the battleship as the final arbiter of battles. A special group TG 58.7 was formed as a battle line, under Vice-Admiral Lee, with *Washington*, *North Carolina*, *Iowa*, *New Jersey*, *South Dakota*, *Alabama* and *Indiana*. No battleship was to come within 300 miles of an opponent, and one carrier task group had to be detached to escort them.

Both sides knew that a climactic moment in the Pacific War was approaching. From Japan, Toyoda made the Nelsonian signal that Admiral Togo had made to his fleet before Tsushima thirty-eight years earlier: 'The fate of the Empire rests on this one battle. Every man is expected to do his utmost.'

In carrier warfare a great advantage goes to the commander who sights his enemy first. Although the Americans were superior to the Japanese in so many ways, in one vital department, sea search, they were markedly inferior. In general, TF 58's air reconnaissance flights were too few, wrongly aimed, and stopped far too short. Spruance's main informants were submarines. *Redfin* reported Ozawa's sailing from Tawi Tawi on 13 June. On the 15th *Flying Fish* reported the Japanese fleet entering the Philippine Sea at almost the same time as *Seahorse* sighted and reported Ugaki's two giant battleships steaming north to join Ozawa. So Spruance knew that the Japanese were in at least two groups, which matched their previous handling of their ships. The next day *Cavalla* reported part of the Japanese fleet. A report from direction-finders on Pearl Harbor reported that the enemy were some 350 miles west-south-west of Spruance on 18 June.

At this, Mitscher suggested that TF 58 steam to the west, so as to be ready to strike early on the 19th. But still Spruance hesitated, and eventually rejected the idea. His orders were to capture, occupy and defend Saipan, Tinian and Guam, and he allowed nothing, neither the glorious but uncertain prospect of destroying the Japanese fleet, nor the risk of being shuttle-bombed by Japanese aircraft taking off from carriers, attacking the American fleet and landing ashore, to deflect him from that duty. Spruance decided to stay near Saipan and so lessen the risk of Japanese forces steaming round him in the night and attacking the landing force off Saipan. In the event, Spruance had TF 58 perfectly placed to take the Japanese onslaught when it came.

Meanwhile, Ozawa had much clearer information of his adversary. On 18 June three of TF 58's groups had been sighted and reported at ranges of 400 miles. Ozawa turned south to keep this distance, which was within range of his own aircraft but beyond the range of the Americans. Rear-Admiral Suoe Obayashi, the carrier admiral in Kurita's Van Force, had prepared a strike of sixty-seven aircraft on his own initiative and had begun to launch them late on the 18th, but the strike was cancelled when Ozawa signalled that the main attacks would be made in the morning. This was a lost opportunity for the Japanese. A strike at dusk might well have caught TF 58 off balance.

At 4.45 a.m. on 19 June, well before dawn, Ozawa began flying off searchers. Some were soon shot down but others successfully reported parts of TF 58's great array of ships and by 8.30 a.m. Obayashi was flying off the first Japanese strike of the day, of sixteen Zekes as escort, forty-five Zekes armed with bombs and eight Jills with torpedoes. Since early that morning, Mitscher's Hellcats had been strafing the airfields of Saipan, Tinian and Guam, shooting down any aircraft they found in the air and destroying any they saw on the ground. With the aircraft the Japanese had already lost, the shorebased 'anvil' on which Ozawa and the Japanese High Command had placed such faith was shattered before the battle even opened.

At about 9 a.m. Ozawa began launching a second strike, a massive one of 128 aircraft: 53 Judys, 27 Jill torpedo-bombers and 48 Zekes. An hour later, a third strike of 47 aircraft followed, and an hour after that, a fourth: another 82 mixed aircraft, 9 Judys, 10 Zekes with bombs, 27 Vals and 6 Jills, with 30 escorting Zekes.

The Japanese were detected by radar up to 150 miles out. With enough time to deploy their fighters, the direction

A Japanese Kate torpedo-bomber
exploding into flames after a direct
hit by a 5 in. shell off Kwajalein,
April 1943

officers of TF 58 had the Hellcats ready, with space and height enough to intercept. It was not a fight, but a massacre. The Hellcat pilots were all experienced men, who had been flying for over two years and had over 300 hours flying time. Their opponents were greenhorns, some of them with less than two months' experience. These were not the veterans of Nagumo's great days; the raw crews broke formation prematurely, failed to press home or co-ordinate their attacks, made elementary errors in station-keeping and left themselves open to the simplest attacking ruses. In the day's aerial combats, which the U.S. sailors later dubbed the 'Great Marianas Turkey Shoot', the Japanese lost 218 of the aircraft in the strikes (the fourth wave lost 72 out of 82). Ozawa finished the day with only 100 aircraft still serviceable. Those that escaped their fate over the fleet flew to Guam or Tinian and were shot down over the airfields there.

Ozawa himself had had an eventful day. That morning, as his flagship *Taiho* had been steaming into wind at 27 knots to launch the first strike, she was hit by one of a salvo of six torpedoes from the U.S. submarine *Albacore*. A second torpedo might have hit but for an extraordinary act of self-sacrifice: Warrant Officer Sakio Komatsu, who had just taken off from *Taiho*'s flight deck, saw a track and exploded the torpedo by diving his Zeke on to it. No serious damage seemed to have been done and *Taiho* steamed on. But the same deadly trail had been laid for her. Petrol pipes had been ruptured, and fumes were distributed round the ship by an inexperienced damage control officer who ordered ventilation fans to be run, hoping that the fumes would be blown overboard. Instead, *Taiho* was filled with petrol fumes, waiting for a spark, like a bomb ready for detonation. It came at 3.32 p.m. that afternoon with an explosion which lifted part of *Taiho*'s flight deck bodily in the air and blew out some of her keel-plates. Ozawa transferred his flag to the cruiser *Haguro*, but only about 500 of *Taiho*'s ship's company of over 2,000 had been saved when there was a colossal explosion and the flagship turned over and sank. She was preceded a few minutes earlier by the veteran carrier *Shokaku*, who had suffered three torpedo hits fired by the submarine *Cavalla* shortly after midday. *Shokaku*, who had been at Pearl Harbor, the Coral Sea and the Eastern Solomons, now went the way of so many Japanese carriers: petrol fumes, fires, huge internal explosions, and the end, just after 3 p.m.

The Japanese pilots had grossly overestimated their claims of American aircraft shot down and American carriers sunk, while Admiral Kukuda, commanding naval aircraft on Tinian, had naturally played down the numbers of his losses. Hampered by meagre communications facilities in *Haguro*,

A Fairey Fulmar taking off from
H.M.S. *Victorious* while the ship is
at anchor

Ozawa had no idea of the extent of the catastrophe which
had befallen his aircrews. Therefore he did not retire, but
stayed in the area, hoping for victory on 20 June. He turned
north-east and his fleet began to refuel.

Mitscher did not fly searches that night of the 19/20th, and
his aircraft did not find Ozawa's ship until 3.40 p.m. on the
afternoon of the 20th. It was late, but not too late. Mitscher
decided to launch an all-out strike of eighty-five Hellcats,
seventy-seven Helldivers and fifty-four Avengers with torpe–
does, taking off at 4.20 p.m., although he knew that many
of the aircraft would not be able to return to their carriers
before dark.

Ozawa broke off his fuelling and prepared for battle again.
Longing for revenge after a day on the defensive, TF 58's

strike brushed aside Ozawa's defence and briskly sank *Hiyo* and two tankers and damaged *Zuikaku* and *Chiyoda*. As their aircraft returned, the Task Force shone searchlights, fired rockets and lit flares to guide them home. Many aircraft crashed in the sea but their crews were picked up, then or next morning. In the two days' action, TF 58 lost seventy-six aircrew and 130 aircraft from all causes. Including their losses of shorebased aircraft, the Japanese lost 476 aircraft, and about 445 aircrew, killed or missing.

Now flying his flag in *Zuikaku*, Ozawa could recognize the true face of defeat. He had only thirty-five aircraft still operational. On his way back to Okinawa, Ozawa offered Toyoda his resignation, who refused it. Spruance pursued until the evening of the 21st, hoping to pick up stragglers and cripples, but realizing that he was losing ground on his fleeing enemy, he called off the pursuit. So ended the Battle of the Philippine Sea, the last and greatest of the carrier battles of the Second World War.

The invasion of Saipan could now go ahead without fear of interruption. The island was declared secured on 9 July. When defeat was inevitable, Admiral Nagumo, C.-in-C. Central Pacific Area with his headquarters on Saipan, was one of the many Japanese who took their own lives. The victor of Pearl Harbor, who had taken Japanese arms to the shores of India, shot himself in a cave and was buried in an unmarked grave. On 11 and 12 July hundreds of Japanese civilians committed a horrifying mass suicide at Marpi Point, in the north of the island. Men cut their own and their wives' throats, parents dashed out their babies' brains, and whole families jumped off the cliffs into the sea to drown.

The nearby islands of Tinian and Guam were invaded on 21 and 24 July (Guam after a saturation bombardment lasting thirteen days) and both islands were secured by the middle of August, although isolated units of Japanese remained at large until the end of the war. (In fact, miserable single survivors of the Japanese armies of the Second World War were still giving themselves up in the 1970s, a quarter of a century later.)

Japanese radio propaganda claimed eleven American carriers sunk in the Philippine Sea, while the successes of *Albacore* and *Cavalla* were not known for some time. So it seemed, for a while, that the battle had not been such a victory after all and there was great disappointment at Pearl Harbor

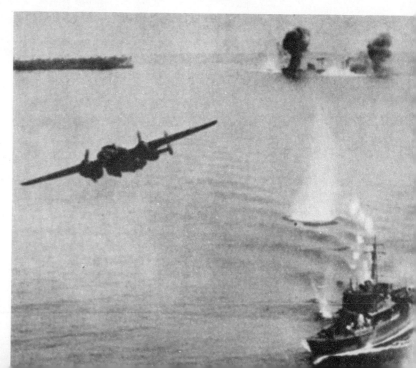

Japanese shipping under attack by B-25 Mitchells off the Philippine coast, 1944

that more Japanese carriers had not been sunk. Even Spruance himself seems to have been persuaded that he might have missed a great opportunity. In fact, by resting on the defensive on 19 June and letting the enemy come to him, Spruance had won a tremendous victory. Had TF 58 struck when Mitscher suggested on the 18th, they might well have expended their force on Kurita's decoy Van Force; Ozawa might then have caught Spruance at a disadvantage with his own strike. Maybe some Japanese carriers had survived, but their aircrews had been decimated, and without pilots the carriers were neutered. That formidable weapon which Nagumo had wielded across half the world had been whittled down to a mere token, to be used as bait in a later battle.

Halsey and Spruance

Such was the pace of events in the Pacific War that no sooner had one operation ended than plans were brought forward for the next. The strain of keeping this constant pressure on the Japanese was such that a dual system of command was evolved in which Spruance and Halsey alternated in command of the fleet. While one admiral and his staff directed one operation, the other admiral and his staff were ashore planning the next. Admiral and staff then relieved each other. The ships were generally the same, but their title changed; the fleet was the Fifth Fleet under Spruance, but became the Third Fleet under Halsey; Task Force 58 became Task Force 38. Thus Spruance commanded the operations in the Gilberts, Marshalls and Marianas, and later at Iwo Jima and the Ryukyus, whilst Halsey commanded in the western Carolines, the Philippines, and in the operations against the Japanese mainland in July and August 1945. It was Halsey in the admiral's chair, having relieved Spruance on 26 August, and it was the Third Fleet at sea when the final confrontation with the Imperial Japanese Navy took place in possibly the greatest sea battle in history, at Leyte Gulf in October 1944.

With Nimitz's forces in the Marianas and MacArthur's at Sansapor on the western tip of New Guinea and already planning an assault on Morotai in the Moluccas, the two prongs of the Allied offensive in the Pacific were only a thousand miles apart, poised to strike next either at the Philippines, or at Formosa. The dispute between the 'Army' and 'Navy' strategies now reached its bitterest stage and, in spite of personal arbitration by President Roosevelt at Pearl Harbor in July 1944, the shape of the final assault on Japan was still unsettled by the time of the Octagon Conference at Quebec in September when, suddenly, the pace of events in the Far East began to accelerate.

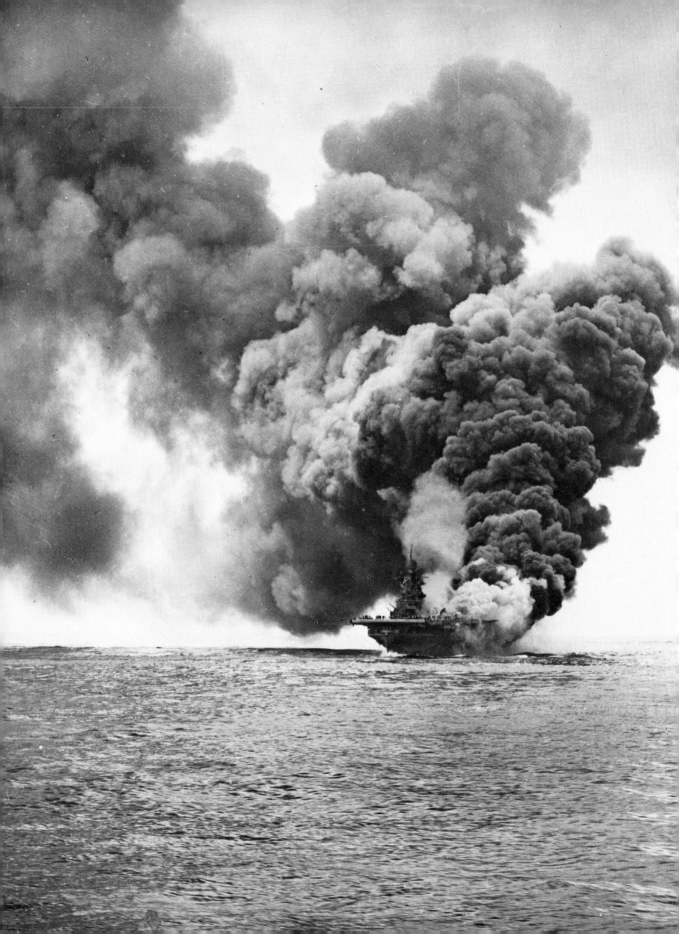

12
Victory over Japan

Build-up to Leyte

Early in September, to support forthcoming landings in the Moluccas and the Palaus, TF 38's aircraft struck at Yap, the Palaus, Mindanao and, from 12 to 14 September, the central Philippine islands, where they met startlingly feeble opposition. About 200 Japanese aircraft were destroyed and several ships sunk, for the loss of eight aircraft from TF 38. Halsey, now convinced that the central Philippines were just a hollow shell with weak defences, urgently suggested to Nimitz that the landings planned for Yap and the Palaus be cancelled and an assault made on Leyte as soon as possible.

The apparent Japanese weakness was due to a planned withdrawal of their resources. They had decided to husband their strength until the Allies were plainly committed to a major offensive in the Philippines. Nimitz agreed to bypass Yap but insisted on the Palaus. After the familiar overture of air strike and bombardment by the Third Fleet, the Marines assaulted the island of Peleliu on 15 September. They met resistance as fierce as any in the Pacific and the island was not secured until early in 1945. But the nearby atoll of Ulithi was taken without opposition on 23 September. Ulithi was a superb natural harbour and became the main forward base for the Third Fleet.

In the Moluccas, MacArthur's forces sidestepped Halmahera, where there was a strong Japanese garrison and landed almost unopposed on Morotai. So by the beginning of October 1944 the Allies held a ring of islands from the Marianas south

The American carrier *Bunker Hill* on fire after a direct hit by a kamikaze off Okinawa, 11 May 1945

Grumman TBF Avenger, the standard torpedo-bomber reconnaissance aircraft of the U.S. Navy from Midway onwards; it later replaced the Barracuda in the Royal Navy. Engine: one 1,900 h.p. Wright R-2600-20 Cyclone radial. Span: 54 ft. 2 in. Length: 40 ft. Maximum speed: 267 m.p.h. at 15,000 ft. Operational ceiling: 23,400 ft. Maximum range: 2,530 miles. Armament: one 0.50 in. machine-gun in each wing and one in the dorsal turret, one 0.303 in. machine-gun in upper engine cowling and one in ventral position; one 22 in. torpedo or one 2,000 lb. bomb

Following pages: The Japanese carrier *Zuiho* under attack by aircraft from *Enterprise* off Cape Engano, 25 October 1944

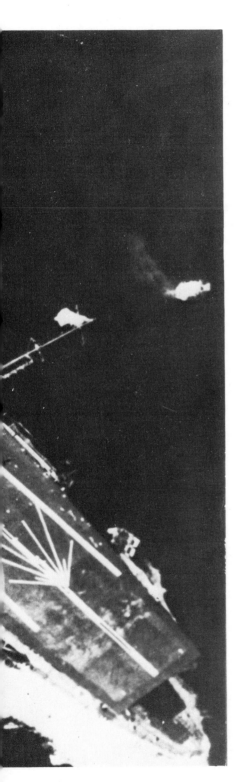

and west to the Moluccas, in an excellent strategic position for an attack on the Philippines.

At Quebec the Joint Chiefs of Staff considered the situation in the light of Halsey's information. With MacArthur's agreement they cancelled the landings on Yap, the Talauds and Mindanao. Nimitz and MacArthur were ordered to join forces for a landing at Leyte on 20 October, two months earlier than the original date set for the Philippine invasion. In an example of the remarkable flexibility of the planning of the Pacific war, a complete Army Corps which was actually on its way to assault Yap was diverted to Manus in the Admiralty Islands to join MacArthur's forces for Leyte. After Leyte, Luzon would inevitably follow. So the long argument between the 'Army' and 'Navy' plans was finally resolved by the passage of events.

The loss of the Philippines would effectively cut off Japan from the resources of the Dutch East Indies and Malaya (for which she had gone to war in the first place). The Japanese had prepared a plan, SHO 1, for the defence of the Philippines. In the Japanese fashion, it required a complicated command structure and the use of decoys.

Battle of Leyte Gulf

On 10 October, TF 38 began preliminary strikes in support of the Leyte landing to come. The attacks were so heavy, with up to 1,000 aircraft taking part, and so widely spread, from the Ryukyus down to the central Philippines, that the Japanese were convinced the main assault had begun. Toyoda prematurely implemented SHO 1 and committed hundreds of naval aircraft to the Philippines. They were very severely mauled by TF 38. In a week the Japanese lost 600 aircraft trying to stop an invasion which had not yet begun.

Since February 1944 the surviving Japanese battleships and most of the heavy cruisers had been at Singapore, to be nearer their supplies of fuel and because their bases in the Palaus and at Truk were untenable. On 18 October Vice-Admiral Takeo Kurita sailed from Lingga Roads, off Singapore, with the First Striking Force of two new and five old battleships, eleven heavy and two light cruisers and nineteen destroyers. After the force had fuelled at Brunei on the 22nd, two battleships under Vice-Admiral Shoki Nishimura were detached to join three cruisers and nine destroyers from Formosa under Vice-Admiral Kiyohide Shima and together form the Second Striking Force. On the 20th Ozawa sailed from Japan with the main body of one fleet carrier, three light carriers, two converted battleship carriers, escorted by three cruisers and eight destroyers. There were no aircraft on board the battleship

The queen of Pacific sea battles, the *Essex* Class aircraft carrier

carriers and only 116, including eighty Zekes, distributed among the other carriers. The Japanese had not been able to train enough fresh aircrews to replace those lost in the Philippine Sea. Ozawa's was a shadow force, sailing on a voyage of self-sacrifice, offering itself as live bait. The Japanese hope was that Halsey would be drawn away from Leyte to attack Ozawa whilst the Japanese capital ships penetrated the Philippine archipelago – Kurita's through the San Bernardino and Nishimura's through the Surigao Strait – to emerge on the eastern side, join forces, and fall upon and destroy the troop anchorages at Leyte.

This time the bait was taken, hook, line, sinker and angler, too. But first the cast.

Early on 23 October, while Kurita's force was still on its way to the Philippines, it was sighted and attacked by the U.S. submarines *Darter* and *Dace* who between them sank the cruisers *Atago*, Kurita's flagship, and *Maya*, and damaged *Takao* so badly she had to return to Singapore. Kurita transferred his flag to *Yamato* and his force steamed on towards the Sibuyan Sea, rounding the southern tip of Mindoro at about 6 a.m. To the south, Nishimura's and Shima's forces were approaching the Mindanao Sea.

On the east of the Philippines lay two vast fleets. The Third Fleet under Halsey had eight fleet and eight light carriers, six battleships, fourteen cruisers and fifty-seven destroyers. The Seventh Fleet, covering the landings under Kinkaid, had another six battleships, eighteen escort carriers, eight cruisers and forty-eight destroyers. Combined, the two fleets made up an enormous force, more than enough to deal with Kurita and Nishimura, provided the force could be applied in the right place.

Task Force 38 was deployed in four groups, three in line 125 miles apart east of the Philippines, and the fourth on its way to Ulithi to refuel. TF 38's aircraft found and reported accurately Kurita's and Nishimura's forces soon after dawn on the 24th, but no searches were flown to the north where Ozawa, having been missed by U.S. submarines, was standing on southwards expecting, indeed hoping, to be detected.

Now that the enemy had been found, Halsey concentrated his three task groups and recalled the fourth from fuelling. Admiral Fukudome, commanding the Japanese naval air forces in the Philippines, had decided that he could best help Kurita by attacking the American carriers. Many of his aircraft were shot down, but at 9.40 a.m. the light carrier *Princeton* was hit by one bomb which penetrated to the hangar: American carriers were sometimes as vulnerable to fires and internal explosions as the Japanese, and *Princeton* had to be sunk later. Meanwhile, Kurita's ships in the Sibuyan Sea had no air cover at all when they came under repeated attacks by TF 38's aircraft, concentrated on the two monster battle-ships *Yamato* and *Musashi*. The American aircrews over-estimated their successes but they made no mistake about *Musashi*, sinking her with about twenty torpedo hits and forty bomb hits. At 3 p.m. Kurita reversed course.

Ozawa launched his token strike at 11.15 a.m. His pilots were so inexperienced they could not land again on flight decks but had to land ashore. Many were shot down, and none of them made a successful attack. But their presence puzzled Halsey, who could not understand why no Japanese carriers had been reported. He ordered Rear-Admiral Sherman, commanding Task Group 38.3, to search to the north, but Sherman was under such heavy air attack that he could not comply until 2 p.m. and it was not until 4.40 p.m. that Ozawa was found at last, about 200 miles to the north-east. It was too late to launch a strike at him before dark, but Halsey decided that Ozawa was his main target and he would attack him in the morning, using all four task groups. The bait had been taken.

That afternoon Halsey signalled to his ships that he intended to form a special task force of battleships and cruisers to oppose Kurita off the eastern entrance to the San Bernardino Strait. Halsey meant that he *would*, but Kinkaid, who intercepted the message, understood that he *had*. So when Halsey took his ships north the entrance of the Strait was not only left uncovered but Kinkaid thought it was covered. (Throughout the battle, communications delays and misunderstandings continued to make matters more difficult for the American commanders.)

That night Nishimura steamed into a deadly trap in the Surigao Strait. Worried by PT boats, attacked and thrown into confusion by destroyers, Nishimura's ships finally ran into the steel wall of battleships and cruisers under Rear-Admiral J. F. Oldendorf, drawn up across the eastern end of the Strait. Nishimura's two battleships were sunk. Nishimura himself was drowned. Only one destroyer of his force escaped un-damaged.

Above: Admiral Jisaburo Ozawa,
who commanded the Japanese
carriers in the Battle of Leyte Gulf

Right: The carrier *Franklin* listing
badly off Luzon, October 1944. The
ship seems about to capsize, but by
superb damage control she
eventually reached Pearl Harbor

The destruction of Nishimura and his pilots' exaggerations of their successes against Kurita earlier in the day convinced Halsey that there would be no danger in leaving San Bernadino unguarded whilst he dealt with Ozawa. In fact Kurita, by no means crushed, had turned east again. At midnight, while Halsey was speeding north, Kurita and his four remaining battleships were passing through the empty straits. By 7 a.m. they were in range of the troop anchorages, which were protected only by a light screen of escort carriers under Rear-Admiral Clifton Sprague.

Sprague's ships put up an outstandingly gallant defence, with bomb and torpedo attacks, smoke screens and a general show of defiance. Nevertheless the destruction of the force seemed inevitable, when Kurita faltered, mistook the escort carriers for fleet carriers, overestimated the forces against him, and turned away. The great prize for which the Imperial Japanese Navy had sacrificed so much was lost. Kurita himself had had his flagship sunk under him, and had been under fierce air attack for three days. As Churchill magnanimously said of him, 'Those who have endured a similar ordeal may judge him.'

Kinkaid had been growing increasingly uneasy about the situation off San Bernardino. Sprague's appeals for help came as a terrible awakening. Kinkaid ordered Oldendorf north to assist Sprague, although he was short of ammunition and unlikely to be there in time, and appealed, sometimes in plain language, to Halsey to come back and help. At Pearl Harbor, Nimitz too was alarmed by the trend of events and signalled to Halsey 'Where is Task Force 34?' Most unfortunately, by another communications mishap, the wording of the signal appeared as an insult, and Halsey took it as such.

Halsey had formed his special Task Force 34 of battleships and cruisers at 4.30 a.m. that morning of 25 October, to attack Ozawa, not Kurita. Halsey was well ahead of his carriers and almost in range of Ozawa when Kinkaid's appeals reached him. Halsey's flagship *New Jersey* was actually only forty miles from the enemy when at 11.15 a.m. Halsey decided to turn back. If it had been right to go after Ozawa, it was wrong to turn away now, but Halsey did so. A Japanese decoy had at last succeeded in splitting the American fleet. Halsey was summoned away from Ozawa and was far too late to catch Kurita. His ships had steamed 600 miles, first north and then south, without engaging the enemy at either end.

But Ozawa did not escape. Mitscher, who had thought of himself as something of a 'passenger' until then, launched strikes that afternoon which sank *Zuikaku*, the last remaining villain of Pearl Harbor, and the light carriers *Zuiho* and *Chitose*. Cruisers finished off *Chiyoda*, which had been

damaged by air attacks that morning. The two battleship-carriers *Ise* and *Hyuga* were both damaged but escaped. These actions, off Cape Engano on the 25th, ended the main battle of Leyte Gulf.

Halsey was bitterly disappointed. 'I turned my back,' he said, 'on the opportunity I had dreamed of since my days as a cadet.' However, errors and omissions accepted, Leyte Gulf was the end of the Imperial Japanese Navy as a fighting force at sea. They had lost three battleships, four carriers, ten cruisers and nine destroyers, with a long added list of ships damaged, some of them put out of the war for good. The Allies lost the carrier *Princeton*, two escort carriers *St Lo* and *Gambier Bay*, three destroyers, the submarine *Darter* which ran aground and was abandoned, and one PT boat.

H.M.S. *Illustrious* after a kamikaze attack off the Sakishima Gunto, April 1945

Kamikaze

St Lo was one of Admiral Sprague's little carriers who had so
gallantly repulsed Kurita off Leyte. She was the first ship to be
lost to a new and ominous form of attack, born of desperation,
which the Japanese used in earnest for the first time against
St Lo and her sister carriers on the morning of 25 October.
From time to time since the earliest days of the war, Japanese
aircraft had crashed into Allied ships in the heat of an action.
Sometimes it had seemed as though the pilot had always
intended, from the moment he took off, to sacrifice himself;
on 15 October, off Luzon, a lone Judy piloted by Rear-
Admiral Masafumi Arima, commanding the 26th Air Flotilla,
had crashed with a 500 lb bomb on the flight deck of the fleet
carrier *Franklin*, damaging her so badly she had to be
withdrawn from the Third Fleet. But there was something
eerily sinister about the way these new attacks were organized;
it was as though the Japanese had begun to use landbased
aircraft as humanly guided missiles to substitute for their lack
of carriers at sea – which indeed they were. The suicide aircraft
had the name Kamikaze, or 'divine wind', called after an old
legend of the Wind-God Ise who on 14 and 15 August 1281 had
saved Japan by raising a typhoon to disperse a great Sino-
Mongol invasion fleet of 3,500 ships assembled by Kublai
Khan. The new units were formed by Vice-Admiral Takajiro
Onishi, who had arrived in Luzon to command the 1st Air
Fleet on 17 October, and were taken from the 201st Air
Group, led on their first sortie by Lieutenant Yukio Seti. The
heavy cruiser H.M.A.S. *Australia* was hit on 21 October; a
much larger attack on the 25th sank *St Lo* and badly damaged
six other escort carriers. From then onwards hardly a day
passed without kamikaze sorties by single planes or by small
groups of up to half a dozen. By the end of January, the
kamikazes from the Philippines had flown 421 sorties, and had
lost 378 of their number; but they had sunk sixteen ships,
including another escort carrier *Ommanney Bay*, and had
damaged another eighty-seven ships, amongst them twenty-
two carriers, five battleships, ten cruisers and twenty-eight
destroyers or destroyer-escorts.

At first the Allied fleet simply could not believe the nature
of their new opponents. Halsey himself was scornful and
incredulous. 'I think,' he said, 'that most of us took it as a sort
of token terror, a tissue-paper dragon. The psychology behind
it was too alien to ours: Americans, who fight to live, find it
hard to realize that other people will fight to die.'[21] However,
Halsey was 'violently disillusioned' the next day, when
kamikazes hit *Belleau Wood* and *Franklin* (again) killing 158
men and knocking both carriers out of the battle line. The

Above: Chance Vought F4U Corsair on deck: the U.S. Navy had difficulty at first in landing these large fighters on flight decks, but Corsairs performed well ashore, flown by the U.S. Marines. Later they saw service as combat fighter and ground-strafing aircraft with the British Pacific Fleet. Engine: one 2,000 h.p. Pratt and Whitney R-2800-8 Double Wasp radial. Span: 40 ft. 11¾ in. Length: 33 ft. 4½ in. Maximum speed: 417 m.p.h. at 19,900 ft. Operational ceiling: 36,900 ft. Normal range: 1,015 miles. Armament: three 0.50 in. Brownings in each wing

Opposite above: The vulnerability of the Seafire: though an excellent fighter in the air, the Seafire had a very bad record of deck crashes

Right: The end in sight: Avengers and Corsairs ranged aft on *Formidable* during attacks on the Japanese mainland, July 1945

Ships of Task Force 38 in line ahead,
December 1944

Allies' incredulity turned to disgust; to western minds there was something unutterably repellent about the way these Japanese pilots were immolating themselves. They could not believe that they were volunteers. By western thinking, they had to be forced. Postwar interrogation confirmed the incredulity of the Allied interrogators and the defiant pride of the kamikaze survivors.

After Leyte Gulf Halsey was able to operate in the Far East with a sublime freedom nobody had had since Nagumo three years before. His ships entered the South China Sea, where no Allied surface warships had operated since 1942. His aircraft ranged freely over targets in Formosa, Hong Kong, and the Japanese held ports of the China coast from Hainan to Amoy and Swatow. When the Third Fleet returned to Ulithi on 25 January 1945 and Halsey was relieved by Spruance, the Third Fleet claimed to have destroyed over 7,000 Japanese aircraft, sunk over ninety Japanese warships of various kinds and nearly 600 merchant ships of a million tons.

Iwo Jima

In February the Third Fleet was once more at sea to give support to the U.S. Marines' assault on Iwo Jima on the 19th. The island was needed for advanced airfields for the air offensive against Japan. Japanese resistance there has become legendary. The Marines had to take the island yard by yard and suffered casualties of 5,931 men killed or died of wounds, and 17,272 wounded; the defending Japanese had 22,000 killed and 867 taken prisoner. The fleet had only one kamikaze attack, on the 21st, but it was a serious one; thirty-two aircraft from Katori in Japan, refuelling at Hachijo Jima, hit and sank the escort carrier *Bismarck Sea* and damaged five other ships, including the old fleet carrier *Saratoga*.

For obvious reasons it was hard for the Japanese to evaluate the effect of their kamikaze campaign. There were few survivors, few accurate reports of damage actually done and, as the grim U.S. Navy joke said, there was no such thing as an experienced kamikaze pilot. Curiously, the suicide units always overestimated the number of ships sunk, but underestimated the number damaged.

Okinawa

For their next and much larger campaign, which began when the U.S. 10th Army landed on Okinawa on 1 April 1945, the Japanese introduced some new tactics. The duel between ships and kamikazes off Okinawa actually began much earlier than the assault landing. On 11 March one of twenty-four

U.S. Marines examining a captured
Yokosuka MXY-7 Ohka (Cherry
Blossom) piloted suicide aircraft
on Ryukyu Island, Okinawa. They
were called 'Baka' (foolish) by the
Americans, but there was nothing
foolish about their attacks. First
flown in numbers off Okinawa in
April 1945, the Ohka was carried
to within twenty miles of its target
in the belly of a parent-bomber
before being launched on its dive.
Engine: one 1,765 lb. type 4 Model
20 solid-propellant rocket motor.
Span: 16 ft. 4 in. Length 19 ft. 11 in.
Maximum level speed: 534 m.p.h.
Maximum diving speed: 621 m.p.h.
Normal range: 55 miles

kamikazes damaged the carrier *Randolph* and on the 18th a group of forty aircraft hit *Intrepid* (again, and for the third time by a kamikaze). On the 21st the Japanese introduced a new rocket-propelled bomber called Ohka, 'Cherry Blossom', (but 'Baka' 'foolish' by the Americans). The Ohkas were really piloted bombs, carried to within twenty miles of their targets in the belly of a Betty bomber. Once launched they achieved speeds of up to 500 m.p.h. and were virtually uninterceptible. Luckily for the Third Fleet, Ohkas had almost no success.

By the end of March, the kamikazes were flying every day. In a massive Ten-Go operation on the 26th, nine U.S. ships including the battleship *Nevada* were damaged. On the 29th Spruance's flagship the heavy cruiser *Indianapolis* was hit and the fleet commander had to transfer his flag to the battleship *New Mexico*, which was later hit herself more than once. The Japanese were relying on the sheer weight of numbers, reasoning that if the fleet's defences were swamped some kamikazes were sure to get through. In thirty-six hours of 6/7 April, the Japanese launched the first attack of their picturesquely named *kikusui* or 'floating chrysanthemum' campaign. No less than 355 kamikazes took off for the attack and although nearly 200 of them were shot down, they sank the destroyers *Bush* and *Calhoun* and two other ships, and damaged twenty-five more. They hit the carrier *Hancock* and the battleship *Maryland* twice on 7 April.

Battle of the East China Sea

As part of the April *kikusui* offensive, the Imperial Japanese Navy made its last sortie in the Pacific War. A naval force under Rear-Admiral Ito, which included *Yamato*, the light cruiser *Yahagi* and eight destroyers, left the Inland Sea on the afternoon of 6 April. The ships had embarked the last stocks of fuel remaining to the Navy which was barely enough to get them to Okinawa. Their plan was to draw off some of the weight of the attack on Okinawa's defenders and, if possible, to beach the ships on Okinawa where their ship's companies could join the defending troops. Their sortie was, in fact, a kamikaze attack on an Homeric scale.

The force was sighted by U.S. submarines that evening, and air searches found it again south of Kyushu at 8.22 a.m. the next morning. At 10 a.m. from a position north-east of Okinawa Mitscher launched a huge strike of 380 dive-bombers and torpedo-bombers, at a range of 250 miles. They found the Japanese ships steaming south shortly after midday. Under repeated attacks the Japanese formation disintegrated. *Yahagi* was overwhelmed by bombs and torpedoes and sunk. The great *Yamato*, whose very name was a sacred one in Japan, followed at 2.25 p.m. after more than a dozen torpedo and bomb hits. *Yamato*'s predicament, in this Battle of the East China Sea, oddly resembled *Prince of Wales*'s years before. Admiral Yamamato, when once asked how aircraft could sink battleships, had replied 'with torpedo-bombers. The fiercest serpent can be overcome by a swarm of ants.'[22] It was true enough. Only four of the destroyers reached Japan.

Under pressure of constant kamikaze attacks the fleet off Okinawa devised defensive tactics of their own. Radar picket destroyers were stationed up to sixty miles from the main fleet in the likeliest direction of attack, to give early warning, and often to bear the first brunt of the suicide attacks. The anti-aircraft armament of ships was doubled and redoubled, and much greater use was made of close proximity shell fuses, to reinforce the fleet's main defence, which was still skilled and determined fighter opposition. Nevertheless the divine wind, as the Americans said, kept coming. Georges Blond, an observer in *Enterprise*, saw an attack on 14 May. 'The deck was deserted: every man, with the exception of the gunners, was lying flat on his face. Flaming and roaring, the fireball passed in front of the island and crashed with a terrible impact just behind the for'ard lift. The entire vessel was shaken, some forty yards of the flight deck folded up like a banana skin; an enormous portion of the lift, at least a third of the platform, was thrown over three hundred feet into the air.'[23]

Japanese survivors clinging to the hull of their destroyer sunk by U.S. aircraft off Okinawa, June 1945

Following pages: **The flight deck of U.S.S.** *Saratoga* **after a kamikaze attack off Iwo Jima, February 1945**

In *Formidable*, on 4 May, an eye-witness said the 'light from above changed to bright orange', and when he went up on deck he saw 'the bridge windows seemed to gape like eye-sockets and much of the island superstructure was blackened'.[24]

The British Pacific Fleet

Formidable was at that time one of four carriers operating with the British Pacific Fleet, which had been formed after considerable political manoeuverings and uncertainties in November 1944. The C.-in-C. was Admiral Sir Bruce Fraser, with his headquarters in Sydney. The fleet was commanded at sea by Vice-Admiral Sir Bernard Rawlings and the carrier squadron was commanded by Vice-Admiral Sir Philip Vian. It was appropriate that the Royal Navy re-entered the Pacific war at sea with air power. Apart from their contribution to the war effort, the Navy itself was keen to try its hand at this new, fast-moving, long-ranging carrier warfare in the Pacific. The fleet had carried out strikes against oil refineries in Sumatra on its way out to Australia in January 1945 and was now off Okinawa operating alongside the Fifth Fleet for the first time. The British Pacific Fleet was given the name of a task force, designated TF 57, although its size of four carriers and escort of battleships and cruisers was really no bigger than the average American task group. The B.P.F.'s task in the capture of Okinawa was the secondary one of

neutralizing the airfields on the islands of the Sakishima Gunto chain, to prevent the Japanese staging aircraft reinforcements through them from Formosa.

The British carriers were not so heavily armed with anti-aircraft guns as the Americans'. They were, in the American phrase, not 'able to look after themselves'. All the carriers in the B.P.F. were hit by kamikazes at one time or another, but they had the inestimable advantage of having armoured flight decks. Aircraft could be operated from the flight deck within hours (once within ninety minutes) of an attack. As a U.S. Navy liaison officer once said, 'When a kamikaze hits a U.S. carrier, it's six months' repair in Pearl. In a Limey carrier, it's "Sweepers, man your brooms".'[25]

Successive *kikusui* waves contained less and less aircraft. The tenth and last, on 21 June, had only forty-five. All sustained terrible losses, of between sixty and ninety per cent shot down. The flying skill of the pilots, never high, sank further until the kamikazes were being flown by raw recruits, farmers and university students, who could barely hold their aircraft in the sky. They could not navigate and had to be shepherded towards their targets by more experienced pilots, who controlled the attacks by radio, in 'Gestapo' planes as they were called. The best kamikaze approaches were either very low so that opposing fighters had less room for manoeuvre, or very high at 25,000 feet, above flak and most interceptors. But the kamikaze pilots had not the skill for either of these tactics and normally flew at average heights, on steady courses and speeds, where they were simply chopped out of the sky. Towards the end, the Japanese used obsolete trainers and slow floatplanes. The main bodies had to conform to these slow speeds, which made them even easier to intercept.

But still the hot wind of destruction kept on blowing. The campaign on land was much harder than had been expected. The carrier task force was forced to operate close offshore against a hostile air arm for far longer than it had been designed to do. The losses mounted daily. Mitscher's own flagship *Bunker Hill* was hit and late in May TF 58 had to be reorganized in three instead of four groups because there were not enough carriers still operational. Kamikaze attacks placed an additional strain on the ship's companies. Ships could never relax, were never safe, from these insane, almost unstoppable attackers. Even when a kamikaze had flown past a ship it might still turn again and dive on deck. The kamikaze pilots were unpredictable and their wholly irrational means of attack seemed to have no rational form of defence.

By the time Okinawa was declared secured on **21 June**, the kamikazes had flown **1,809** sorties and lost **930** aircraft. They had sunk seventeen ships and damaged 198, including

Two blisters that glare straight ahead
  like bulls-eyes,
A flat wing with a knob at each tip,
A hull squashed so flat as to cause
  great surprise
At the things Catalina can ship.

twelve carriers and ten battleships. In all kamikaze operations, the Japanese Navy flew 2,314 sorties and lost 1,228 aircraft. They sank thirty-four ships and damaged the staggering number of 288.

Operations off Japan

On 10 July the Third Fleet, once more under Halsey, began operations off the Japanese mainland with exploratory strikes against airfields on the Tokyo plain. These were preliminaries, to keep unremitting pressure on the Japanese before the landings on the Japanese home islands which were planned for November 1945. On the 16th TF 38 was joined by TF 37, the British Pacific Fleet under Admiral Rawlings, which operated to all intents and purposes as part of the U.S. Fleet. Halsey now commanded the greatest and most powerful fleet in naval history. The Third Fleet, organized in three task groups, had ten fleet and six light carriers, with 1,191 aircraft, eight battleships, nineteen cruisers and over sixty destroyers. The British, with four fleet carriers and 255 aircraft, the battleship *King George V*, six cruisers and fifteen destroyers, took an honoured position on the right of the line. They struck comparatively blow for blow with the Americans until the end, although they were constantly hampered by their lack of enough fast tankers and supply ships in the fleet train.

The Third Fleet's operations off Japan in July and August 1945 were the most polished professional aerial performances of the war at sea. This was the consummation of the carrier art. The great fleet turned and wheeled as one, concentrating to strike, dispersing to fuel, shuttling up and down the coast of Japan at will, advancing and retreating as one great supple weapon. The fleet was able to use several modes of modern warfare: air strike, with gun, bomb and torpedo, played its part with battleship bombardment, surface sweeps by cruisers and destroyers, radio deception, submarine operations and mining.

The fleet's tasks were to reduce the enemy's tactical naval and army air forces, to attack strategic targets on the Japanese mainland, and to probe the strength of the Japanese defences in northern Honshu and Hokkaido which were both beyond reasonable range of aircraft from the Marianas. These tasks were amended during the operations to include the destruction of the remnants of the Japanese Navy and Japanese merchant shipping.

Task Force 38 found enemy opposition surprisingly light. As in the Philippines, the Japanese had decided to hoard their strength until the Allies had committed themselves to a landing, and the fleet's main adversary was the weather which prevented or curtailed flying operations on several days. TF 38 carried out thirteen strike days (TF 37: eight days) and three heavy bombardments. They destroyed or damaged 2,408 aircraft (TF 37: 347) and sank or damaged 924,000 tons of Japanese shipping (TF 37: 356,760 tons).

The surviving heavy ships of the Japanese Navy were immobilized for lack of fuel and were lying heavily camouflaged and reduced to the status of floating anti-aircraft batteries, the battleship *Nagato* at Yokosuka and the rest at Kure on the Inland Sea. In three days' strikes the Third Fleet's aircraft sank or damaged *Nagato*, the battleships *Ise*, *Haruna* and *Hyuga*, the aircraft carrier *Amagi*, the cruisers *Tone*, *Aoba*, *Iwate* and *Izumo* and many other lesser ships in a final revenge for Pearl Harbor. Somewhat ungenerously, the Americans excluded the British air groups from these strikes, giving them secondary targets on those days.

On 9 August, *Formidable*'s Corsair squadrons were striking at airfields and shipping along the coast of Honshu. One strike was led by the Senior Pilot of 1841 Squadron, Lt. Robert Hampton Gray D.S.C., R.C.N.V.R., a Canadian from Nelson, British Columbia, and one of the most aggressive and skilful pilots in the fleet. He had taken part in the strikes against *Tirpitz* in 1944 and had just won his D.S.C. for his service in the Sakishima Gunto earlier that year. Gray's aircraft was carrying a 1,000 lb bomb, which he decided to drop on a Japanese destroyer lying camouflaged close alongside the shore. Gray pressed home his attack through very heavy flak and sank the destroyer, but he himself was killed. In November he was awarded a posthumous V.C. In a sense it was one of the saddest awards of the war. The struggle was so nearly over. The first atomic bomb had been dropped on Hiroshima. Blockade by sea and incessant attack from the air had brought Japan down and she was within days of surrender. The cause for which Gray gave his life was already won.

After the war was over the fleets were the only Allied force instantly available to accept the Japanese surrenders and to begin at once the work of postwar rehabilitation. But first the air groups indulged in a pardonable piece of showing off. On 22 August, while the fleet was waiting to enter Tokyo Bay, the aircraft of the Third Fleet carried out Operation Tintype, massing overhead in hundreds and flying past the fleet. There were over a thousand aircraft in the sky at once, their wings seeming to stretch from horizon to horizon. One by one the squadrons roared overhead, dipping and rolling in salute above the waving thousands below. On 2 September 1945, when the instrument of surrender was signed on board the battleship *Missouri*, the carriers who had so often held the ring in war stayed at sea while peace was made.

The Battle of the East China Sea,
April 1945 : the giant Japanese
battleship *Yamato* hit by a bomb
and later sunk

Select Bibliography

APPLEMAN, Roy E., BURNS, James M., GUGLER, Russell A., and STEVENS, John, *United States Army in World War Two: War in the Pacific, Okinawa, Last Battle* (Historical Division, Department of the Army, Washington 1948).

CHURCHILL, Winston S., *The Second World War* (Cassell, London 1948–54), 6 vols.

CUNNINGHAM OF HYNDHOPE, Admiral of the Fleet, Viscount, *A Sailor's Odyssey* (Hutchinson, London 1951).

DERRY, T. K., *The Campaign in Norway* (H.M.S.O., London 1952).

FRERE-COOK, Gervis, *The Attack on the 'Tirpitz'* (Ian Allen, London 1973).

FUCHIDA, M., and OKUMIYA, M., *Midway: The Battle That Doomed Japan* (Hutchinson, London and U.S. Naval Institute, Annapolis, 1957).

HALSEY, Admiral William, and BRYAN III, J., *Admiral Halsey's Story* (McGraw-Hill, New York 1947).

HOUGH, Richard, *The Hunting of Force Z* (Collins, London 1963).

INOGUCHI, Rikihei, NAKAJIMA, Tadashi, and PINEAU, Roger, *The Divine Wind* (U.S. Naval Institute, Annapolis 1958).

ITO, Masanori, *The End of the Imperial Japanese Navy* (Weidenfeld and Nicolson, London and W. W. Norton and Co., New York, 1962).

KENNEDY, Ludovic, *Pursuit: Sinking of the 'Bismarck'* (Collins, London 1974).

LORD, Walter, *Day of Infamy* (Longmans, Green and Co., London 1957 and Bantam Books, New York 1963).

MACARTHUR, General of the Army, Douglas, *Reminiscences* (Heinemann, London 1964).

MACINTYRE, Donald, *The Battle of the Atlantic* (Batsford, London 1961).

MINISTRY OF INFORMATION, *Coastal Command* (H.M.S.O., London 1943).
—— *The Fleet Air Arm* (H.M.S.O., London 1943).

MORISON, Samuel Eliot, *The History of United States Naval Operations in World War Two* (Oxford University Press, Oxford and Little, Brown and Co., Boston, 1947–59), 15 vols.

NEWCOMB, Richard F., *Savo* (Holt, Rinehart and Winston, New York 1961).

POTTER, E. B., and NIMITZ, Fleet Admiral Chester W., *The Great Sea War* (Harrap, London and Prentice-Hall, New Jersey, 1961).

POTTER, John Deane, *Fiasco: The Break-Out of the German Battleships* (Heinemann, London 1970).

Purnell's History of the Second World War (London 1969–72), 8 vols.

ROSKILL, Captain S. W., *The War at Sea 1939–1945* (H.M.S.O., London 1954), 3 vols.

SMITH, Peter C., *Pedestal: The Malta Convoy of August 1942* (William Kimber, London 1970).

VIAN, Admiral Sir Philip, *Action This Day* (Muller, London 1960).

WOHLSETTER, Roberta, *Pearl Harbor* (Stanford University Press, 1962).

WOODWARD, C. V., *The Battle for Leyte Gulf* (Macmillan Publishing Co., New York 1947).

Notes

1. Captain S. W. Roskill, *The War at Sea 1939–1945*, vol.1 (H.M.S.O., London 1954).
2. Ronald Healiss, *Adventure 'Glorious'* (Muller, London 1955).
3. Lt. M. R. Maund R.N., 'A Taranto Diary', *Blackwoods Magazine*.
4. ibid.
5. Don Newton and A. Cecil Hampshire, *Taranto* (William Kimber, London 1959).
6. Donald MacIntyre, *The Battle for the Mediterranean* (Batsford, London 1964).
7. Margit Fjellman, *Louis Mountbatten* (Allen and Unwin, London 1968).
8. Ludovic Kennedy, *Pursuit: Sinking of the 'Bismark'* (Collins, London 1974).
9. ibid.
10. W. D. James, ed., *Hamptonians at War* (privately printed for Hampton Grammar School).
11. ibid.
12. M. Okumiya and J. Harikoshi, *Zero!* (Cassell, London 1962).
13. S. E. Morison, 'Coral Sea, Midway and Submarine Actions, May–August 1942', *The History of U.S. Naval Operations in World War Two*, vol. 4 (Little, Brown and Co., New York and Oxford University Press, Oxford, 1950).
14. John Deane Potter, *Fiasco: The Break-Out of the German Battleships* (Heinemann, London 1970).
15. Ministry of Information, *The Fleet Air Arm* (H.M.S.O., London 1943).
16. Lt.-Com. John Moore R.N.V.R., *Escort Carrier* (Hutchinson, London 1944).
17. S. E. Morison, 'The Atlantic Battle Won, May 1943–May 1945', op. cit., vol. 10 (New York 1955 and Oxford 1956).
18. Admiral Sir Philip Vian, *Action This Day* (Muller, London 1960).
19. Hugh Popham, *Sea Flight* (William Kimber, London 1954).
20. Ministry of Information, *Coastal Command* (H.M.S.O., London 1943).
21. Admiral William Halsey and J. Bryan III, *Admiral Halsey's Story* (McGraw-Hill, New York 1947).
22. Richard Hough, *The Hunting of Force Z* (Collins, London 1963).
23. Jean Larteguy, ed., *The Sun Goes Down* (William Kimber, London 1956).
24. Wardroom Officers, H.M.S. *Formidable*, *A Formidable Commission* (Seeley Services, London 1946).
25. John Winton, *The Forgotten Fleet* (Michael Joseph, London 1969).

Index

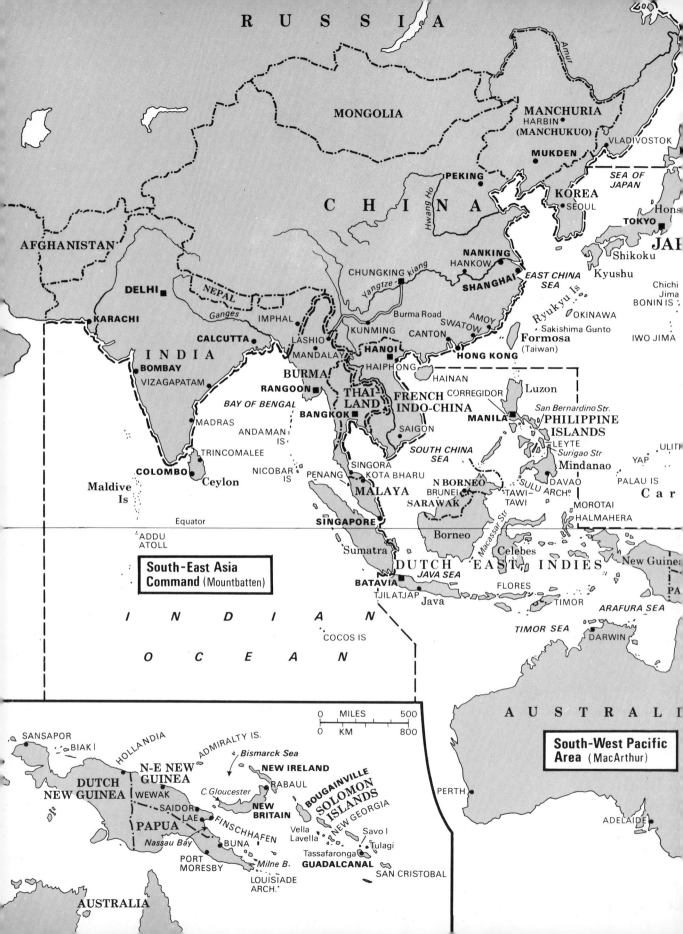

RUSSIA

MONGOLIA

MANCHURIA
(MANCHUKUO)
HARBIN

VLADIVOSTOK

MUKDEN

PEKING

C H I N A

KOREA
SEOUL

SEA OF
JAPAN

Hons

AFGHANISTAN

CHUNGKING
Yangtze- kiang

NANKING
HANKOW

SHANGHAI

EAST CHINA
SEA

TOKYO

JAP

Shikoku

Kyushu

Chichi
Jima
BONIN IS

DELHI

NEPAL

Ganges

IMPHAL

KUNMING

Burma Road

SWATOW

AMOY

Ryukyu Is

OKINAWA

Sakishima Gunto

IWO JIMA

KARACHI

CALCUTTA

LASHIO
MANDALAY

HANOI

CANTON

HAIPHONG

HONG KONG

Formosa
(Taiwan)

I N D I A

BOMBAY

VIZAGAPATAM

RANGOON

THAI-
LAND

BURMA

HAINAN

FRENCH
INDO-CHINA

CORREGIDOR

Luzon

San Bernardino Str.

MANILA

PHILIPPINE
ISLANDS

ULIT

BAY OF BENGAL

MADRAS

ANDAMAN
IS

BANGKOK

SAIGON

SOUTH CHINA
SEA

LEYTE
Surigao Str

YAP

Mindanao

PALAU IS

Car

TRINCOMALEE

NICOBAR
IS

SINGORA
PENANG   KOTA BHARU

MALAYA

N BORNEO
BRUNEI
SARAWAK

SULU ARCH.
TAWI-
TAWI

DAVAO

MOROTAI

HALMAHERA

COLOMBO

Ceylon

Maldive
Is

Equator

ADDU
ATOLL

SINGAPORE

Sumatra

Borneo

Macassar Str

Celebes

New Guinea

PA

South-East Asia
Command (Mountbatten)

DUTCH EAST INDIES

JAVA SEA

BATAVIA

TJILATJAP   Java

FLORES

TIMOR

ARAFURA SEA

I N D I A N

COCOS IS

O C E A N

TIMOR SEA

DARWIN

A U S T R A L I

0   MILES   500
0   KM   800

SANSAPOR

BIAK I

HOLLANDIA

ADMIRALTY IS.

Bismarck Sea

NEW IRELAND

RABAUL

South-West Pacific
Area (MacArthur)

DUTCH
NEW GUINEA

N-E NEW
GUINEA

WEWAK

C. Gloucester

NEW
BRITAIN

BOUGAINVILLE
SOLOMON
ISLANDS

PERTH

SAIDOR
LAE
PAPUA

FINSCHHAFEN

Vella
Lavella

NEW GEORGIA

Savo I

Nassau Bay

BUNA

Tulagi

ADELAIDE

PORT
MORESBY

Milne B.

Tassafaronga

GUADALCANAL

SAN CRISTOBAL

LOUISIADE
ARCH.

AUSTRALIA